The Bluebird Book

The bluebird carries the sky on his back.
— *HENRY DAVID THOREAU*

Stokes Nature Guides

BY DONALD STOKES

A Guide to Nature in Winter
A Guide to Observing Insect Lives
A Guide to Bird Behavior, Volume I

BY DONALD AND LILLIAN STOKES

A Guide to Bird Behavior, Volume II
A Guide to Bird Behavior, Volume III
A Guide to Enjoying Wildflowers
A Guide to Animal Tracking and Behavior

BY THOMAS F. TYNING

A Guide to Amphibians and Reptiles

Stokes Backyard Nature Books

BY DONALD AND LILLIAN STOKES

The Bird Feeder Book
The Hummingbird Book
The Complete Birdhouse Book

Also by Donald Stokes

The Natural History of Wild Shrubs and Vines

THE BLUEBIRD BOOK

THE COMPLETE GUIDE TO ATTRACTING BLUEBIRDS

DONALD and LILLIAN STOKES

Authors of *Stokes Nature Guides*
and *Stokes Backyard Nature Books*

Illustrations by Donald Stokes

Foreword by Sadie Dorber
President, North American Bluebird Society

Little, Brown and Company

Boston   Toronto   London

First edition

"The Last Word of a Bluebird," by Robert Frost, from *The Poetry of Robert Frost,* edited by Edward Connery Lathem. Copyright 1916 © 1969 by Holt, Rinehart and Winston. Copyright 1944 by Robert Frost. Reprinted by permission of Henry Holt and Company, Inc.

Excerpt from "Over the Rainbow." Copyright 1938, 1939 (Renewed 1966, 1967) Metro-Goldwyn-Mayer, Inc., assigned to EMI Catalogue Partnership. All rights controlled and administered by EMI Feist Catalog, Inc. All rights reserved. Used by permission. Composers: Harold Arlen and E. Y. Harburg.

Journal entry, Journal xii, 5, March 2, 1859, by Henry David Thoreau, from *Thoreau's World,* edited by Charles R. Anderson. Copyright © 1971 by Charles R. Anderson. Reprinted by permission of Prentice-Hall, Inc., New Jersey.

"Vanity in Blue" by Allen Eugene Metelman and "Bluebird Honeymoon" by Katharine M. Braun first appeared in *Sialia,* the journal of the North American Bluebird Society. Used by permission of the authors.

Library of Congress Cataloging-in-Publication Data
Stokes, Donald W.
    The bluebird book: the complete guide to attracting bluebirds / Donald and Lillian Stokes; illustrations by Donald Stokes; foreword by Sadie Dorber. — 1st ed.
      p. cm.
     ISBN 0-316-81745-7
     1. Bluebirds. 2. Birds, Attracting of. I. Stokes, Lillian Q. II. Title.
    QL696.P255S76 1991
    598.8′42 — dc20   90-49878

10 9 8 7 6 5 4 3 2 1

RRD-OH

Published simultaneously in Canada by Little, Brown & Company (Canada) Limited

Printed in the United States of America

Acknowledgments
Special thanks to Elsie K. Eltzroth, coordinator of the Audubon Society of Corvallis Bluebird Trail, for her research information on western bluebirds. Thanks also to these bluebird experts for reading the manuscript and offering helpful suggestions: Lawrence Zeleny, Sadie Dorber, Elsie K. Eltzroth, Myrna Pearman, and Donna Hagerman.

Photograph Acknowledgments
Audubon Workshop: 37.
Ron Austing: 56, 67, 71, 72, 82 left.
Carlyle Calvin: 24, 60.
Herbert Clarke: 25.
Bruce Coleman, Inc: Bob and Clara Calhoun — 59; Edgar T. Jones — 63; Roy Morsch — 45; Laura Riley — 46, 87; Leonard Lee Rue III — 51; Joseph Van Wormer — 35; Wardene Weisser — 12.
Joe and Terry Dana: 36.
Bill Duyck: 17, 81, 85.
Merlin S. Eltzroth: 74.
John Findlay III: 40.
Images of Nature: Thomas Mangelsen — 89.
Isidor Jeklin: 1, 11, 14, 33, 42, 54 left, 54 right, 55 top, 55 bottom, 77.
Gordon Johnson: 21, 78.
Maslowski Photo: 19, 27, 32, 57, 69, 93.
David Middleton: 7, 22, 23.
Photo Researchers, Inc.: Richard R. Hansen — 20.
C. Gable Ray: 6, 15, 58, 61, 75, 94.
Carl Sams III: 88.
Gregory K. Scott: 53.
Lorne Scott: 79.
Michael L. Smith: 10, 13, 16, 39, 65, 70, 76, 80, 82 right, 83 left, 84, 91, 92.
Ron Spomer: 62.
Stokes Nature Company: 29, 38, 41, 44, 48, 49, 52, 83 right.
Valan Photo: Dennis W. Schmidt — 8; Robert C. Simpson — 43.
VIREO: S. J. Lang — 9, 64; P. La Tourrette — 18.
Mary F. Zoller: 68, 73.

Range Maps by Dianne B. McCorry.

CONTENTS

FOREWORD

Only a decade ago, bluebirds were an uncommon sight in our rural communities. In fact, many people under the age of forty have never known the joy of seeing bluebirds and hearing their soft warbling song.

This is because the tree holes where bluebirds nest were inadvertently destroyed by human activities. Dead trees, which contain tree holes, were harvested for firewood or taken down because of appearance. Wooden fence posts, in which woodpeckers might hollow cavities that could then be used by bluebirds, were replaced by metal posts and wire. And the few remaining natural nest cavities were often taken over by the more aggressive starlings and house sparrows, introduced from Europe.

The lack of nesting cavities resulted in a severe decline in the population of all three species of bluebirds. The eastern bluebird seemed to have suffered most, and it is estimated that its population plummeted by as much as 90 percent.

The formation of the North American Bluebird Society in 1978 has resulted in the bluebird movement's sweeping across the continent. The primary objective of the society is to educate all who will listen about the importance of preserving these singular creatures in their native habitat. The society provides a central clearinghouse for ideas that help preserve bluebirds, addresses problems that face bluebird trail monitors, and supports and conducts extensive research on all aspects of the preservation and behavior of bluebirds.

One of the results of the bluebird movement has been a tremendous increase in our knowledge about bluebirds. We now know much more about the year-round requirements and behavior of all three species. And we know many more ways to provide better and safer nest boxes and nesting habitats.

Simultaneously with the bluebird movement, public awareness of the environmental problems facing the whole planet has been growing. This has resulted in a renewed interest in helping all wildlife. Bluebirds are one part of our environment that we can easily help, since they readily adapt to man-made cavities in the form of nesting boxes. Their future virtually rests in our hands.

Youth organizations, clubs, and many senior citizens and other individuals have become dedicated to the movement. Some people put up just a few boxes in their own backyards, while others

A male eastern bluebird in all his splendor.

A male western bluebird perched atop a conifer.

have extensive trails of hundreds to even thousands of boxes. All of these "bluebirders" have the same goal — to provide safe nesting sites for bluebirds and other native cavity nesters.

Although the bluebird movement started primarily with interest in the eastern bluebird, it quickly spread to the western and mountain bluebirds as well. Increasing conservation efforts on behalf of these species are being carried out with wonderful results.

Because of all these occurrences, we are now seeing more bluebirds. Bluebirds are nesting where they hadn't for decades. The work of so many interested persons appears to be stabilizing the bluebird populations. Succeeding generations will, we hope, be able to continue to enjoy one of our most beautiful birds.

In their continuing series of Stokes Backyard Nature Books, Don and Lillian Stokes are presenting here *The Bluebird Book*. It combines many features for the first time in one book: excellent summaries of how to attract bluebirds through nest boxes, roosting boxes, bluebird trails, landscaping, and feeders; necessary advice on how to monitor boxes and protect them from predators and competitors; detailed and up-to-date information on the identification, habitat, and behavior of all three species; accounts of the history of bluebird populations and conservation activities; and gorgeous color photographs of the three species of bluebirds, showing all aspects of their lives.

I know that *The Bluebird Book* will add to the knowledge and enjoyment of everyone, from beginners putting up their first nesting box to experienced bluebirders. Let's hope it also leads to more bluebirds for all to enjoy.

Sadie Dorber
President, North American Bluebird Society

THE JOYS OF BLUEBIRDS

Love at First Sight

We were on a country road in Maine, years ago, when we saw our first bluebird — a male perched on a small sugar maple. We knew other people who were crazy about bluebirds and, frankly, we thought they were exaggerating and possibly naive. But on this day in Maine, we realized that no amount of hype could have prepared us for our first look. This bluebird was far more beautiful than we had ever been told.

The mountain bluebird — this one is a male — is easy to enjoy. Beautiful and charming, it lets you get close enough to watch it.

We could not believe the blue. Our breath was taken away, and our eyes were transfixed. It was the bluest blue of any bird we had ever seen, scintillating, the hue of the clearest sunny spring sky. We realized that, as Thoreau said, the bluebird really does carry the sky on its back. Added to the blue was the robin red of the male's breast and the crisp white of his underparts — the perfect counterpoints to that blue. For us, it was love at first sight.

Conservation in Action

Where we live in eastern Massachusetts, bluebirds are rare. But we knew even before we saw one that they were making a comeback thanks to the efforts of bluebirders all across the country. We decided to do what we could to help bluebirds return to our town, where they were practically never seen and had not bred for more than 20 years.

We obtained the financial support and cooperation of our garden club and conservation commission and got a retired friend to help us make nest boxes. In March we ventured out and set up two trails on conservation land and one on our own property.

In the wake of our rising hopes were many disappointments. One year a bluebird pair nested on a trail but inexplicably deserted their eggs and left. The following year, another pair bred, but, despite our monitoring, a nest of 12-day-old young perished after 3 days of cold, torrential rains. We were depressed for days.

Our spirits soared the next year when a pair came to our property and spent three hours exploring the boxes. We keenly watched their every move. The male flitted from box to box, wing-waving (a courtship display) and singing to his recalcitrant mate. Then suddenly the pair flew up

A male eastern bluebird perched on a red tool handle.

over the trees and out of sight. We wished we could have "spoken bluebird" and could have called after them to say that our property would be a safe place to stay and that we would take good care of them. But we had no way to express this and had to accept their choice to move. Meanwhile, tree swallows, titmice, chickadees, and wrens all nested on our trails.

After several failed attempts by other pairs on other trails, we were about to give up. Of course, that was the year we suddenly were blessed with a bonanza of bluebirds — three pairs nested successfully in our town.

Fittingly, as we write this book, a pair is finally nesting in a box on our own property. Did they know we were writing about them? We muse.

Even though we have seen many bluebirds breed elsewhere, there is nothing like having them breed on your own property. We feel like some of the chosen.

Cheerful Charmer

Bluebirds are not only beautiful, they are charming as well. Their large, dark eyes give them an expressive face that usually appears alert and amiable but at times seems grumpy, especially when viewed head on; when tipped to the side to eye a juicy caterpillar, it can even look comic.

The fact that bluebirds nest and feed in the open makes them easy to watch, and their tameness and tolerance of humans is endearing. We especially enjoy seeing the close and seemingly tender relationship between the male and female as he guides her to nesting sites and feeds her during courtship and incubation.

Bluebirds Forever

The return of the bluebird is a remarkable conservation success story. It has happened thanks to thousands of dedicated people all across North America who have seen the bluebird, fallen in love, and wanted to help it survive.

Bluebirds are thriving, but they still need your help. We have written this book to make it easier for you to attract, enjoy, and successfully maintain nesting bluebirds.

May the "bluebird of happiness" enter and always remain in your life.

Don and Lillian Stokes

A CELEBRATION OF BLUEBIRDS

Many people have been inspired by the beauty and character of bluebirds, and this often has led them to write prose, poems, and songs about the birds. Since these expressions are an important display of people's love for bluebirds, we felt that a few samples would be an enjoyable and fitting part of this book.

A male eastern bluebird resting on a tree stump in the afternoon light.

As I went out a Crow
In a low voice said, "Oh,
I was looking for you.
How do you do?
I just came to tell you
To tell Lesley (will you?)
That her little Bluebird
Wanted me to bring word
That the north wind last night
That made the stars bright
And made ice on the trough
Almost made him cough
His tail feathers off.
He just had to fly!
But he sent her Good-by,
And said to be good,
And wear her red hood,
And look for skunk tracks
In the snow with an ax —
And do everything!
And perhaps in the spring
He would come back and sing."

ROBERT FROST
"The Last Word of a Bluebird
(as told to a child)"

Somewhere over the rainbow
Bluebirds fly.
Birds fly over the rainbow —
Why then, oh why can't I?

EDGAR Y. HARBURG
From "Over the Rainbow"
The Wizard of Oz

A male eastern bluebird just landing at the nest with food for his hungry nestlings.

Princes and magistrates are often styled serene, but what is their turbid serenity to that ethereal serenity which the bluebird embodies? His Most Serene Birdship! His soft warble melts in the ear, as the snow is melting in the valleys around. The bluebird comes and with his warble drills the ice and sets free the rivers and ponds and frozen ground. As the sand flows down the slopes a little way, assuming the forms of foliage where the frost comes out of the ground, so this little rill of melody flows a short way down the concave of the sky.

HENRY DAVID THOREAU
Journals — March 2, 1859

A male mountain bluebird at the nest with a variety of insects in his beak.

Come along with me, my love,
  And we will roam the sky;
We'll fly across the meadows,
  And soar o'er mountains high.

We'll drink of streams' pure waters;
  Chase butterflies and bees;
And when we tire of this, my love,
  We'll rest in shady trees.

Then we will search in earnest,
  Each nook and cranny wide;
Where we can raise our family
  Together, side by side.

There it is, my dearest love.
  Well, goodness! Bless my soul!
Just waiting there for us, dear one,
  Our house upon a pole.

A kind and careful craftsman
  Has built it strong and true;
DO enter into it, my love,
  And I will follow you.

KATHARINE M. BRAUN
"Bluebird Honeymoon"

With the first soft, plaintive warble of the bluebirds early in March, the sugar camps, waiting for their signal, take on a bustling activity; the farmer looks to his plough; orders are hurried off to the seedsmen; a fever to be out of doors seizes one: spring is here. Snowstorms may yet whiten fields and gardens, high winds may howl about the trees and chimneys, but the little blue heralds persistently proclaim from the orchard and the garden that the spring procession has begun to move. *Tru-al-ly, tru-al-ly,* they sweetly assert to our incredulous ears.

NELTJE BLANCHAN
From *Bird Neighbors*

O bluebird, welcome back again,
  Thy azure coat and ruddy vest
  Are hues that April loveth best, —
Warm skies above the furrowed plain.

The farm boy hears thy tender voice
  And visions come of crystal days,
  With sugar-camps in maple ways,
And scenes that make his heart rejoice.

The lucid smoke drifts on the breeze,
  The steaming pans are mantling white,
  And thy blue wing's a joyous sight,
Among the brown and leafless trees.

JOHN BURROUGHS
From "The Bluebird"

Blue bird sass de robin,
Robin sass him back,
Den de blue bird scol' him
'Twell his face is black.
Wouldn' min' de quoilin'
All de mo'nin' long,
'Cept it wakes me early,
Case hit's done in song.

PAUL LAURENCE DUNBAR
From "Spring Fever"

A male eastern bluebird.

CherWee! CherWee! CherWee! CherWee!
Look close, my love, and you will see
    I'm animated jewelry,
    Contrived of la-pis la-zu-li
        And other gems of pedigree!

A topaz of the rosiest
Was fashioned for my loving breast,
    My eyes are beads of molten jet,
    With silver reeds my tongue is set!
        Of platinum, my legs and toes
        Excite the envy of my foes!

Oh, let us build, for love serene,
A house of purple velveteen,
    Where I can glow, where I can preen
    The splendor of my cobalt sheen!

    You're somewhat lovely, *too,*
    My queen.

ALLEN EUGENE METELMAN
"Vanity in Blue"

EASTERN BLUEBIRD

Sialia sialis

Identification

Adult Male Plumage — Dark blue on the head, back, wings, and tail. Reddish brown from the chin down over the breast and further back along the flanks. Reddish brown also from the throat back along the sides of the neck. The belly is white.

Adult Female Plumage — Light gray tinged with blue on head. Dull brown on back. Blue on tail and wings seen most when flying and not always apparent when perched. Light reddish-brown color extends from chin over breast and back along flanks. Belly and undertail white. Has a white eye-ring. Some females appear almost all brown, others look much more like the blue males. These differences are individual and not a matter of age.

Juvenal Plumage — Brown to gray on head, back, chin, breast, and along flanks, with white spots overlaying breast and flank. Conspicuous white eye-ring. Wing and tail feathers almost all blue in the male and dull gray-black in the female with only a little blue. The spotted plumage of the body is lost in the post-juvenal molt, which occurs in mid- to late summer.

Subspecies — There is a subspecies of the eastern bluebird (*Sialia sialis fulva*) that lives in the mountains of southeastern Arizona. It is non-migratory and is slightly paler overall.

Distinguishing Eastern Bluebirds from Other Bluebirds

Male — Only the male western bluebird is likely to be confused with the male eastern bluebird, since both have similar patterns of red and blue plumage; the male mountain bluebird is all blue with no red. The most obvious difference between the western and eastern males is their throat and chin. The eastern male has a red-brown throat and chin, whereas the western male has a blue throat and chin. The male eastern also has an all-blue back, whereas the male western has varying amounts of reddish brown on the back.

Female — The female eastern is more two-toned, with reddish brown on front and blue-gray on head and back, while the female mountain bluebird has more uniform gray to blue-gray color on her head, back, and front. The female western bluebird has a pale gray throat rather than reddish as in the female eastern bluebird.

A male eastern bluebird with food, pausing for a moment before delivering it to the nestlings.

A male eastern bluebird watching over his territory.

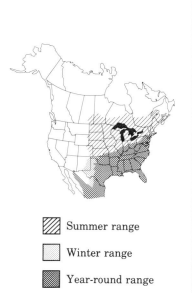

Summer range

Winter range

Year-round range

Hybrids

Mountain and eastern bluebirds have bred together and successfully raised hybrid young. These hybrids (mountain x eastern) have also bred successfully with nonhybrids.

Most hybrids of these two species have been discovered in southwestern Manitoba, Canada. This is one of the broadest areas of range overlap between the two species; it is also a heavily monitored area with a great many nest boxes. Thus, it is hard to determine whether most hybrids occur here or whether the higher numbers are just a result of more observation.

Western and eastern bluebirds only marginally overlap breeding ranges, and to date there are no records of hybridization between these two species in the wild.

Range and Habitat

The eastern bluebird breeds throughout the eastern half of the United States and southern Canada. Populations are sparse in the North but increasing with conservation efforts. Some eastern bluebirds migrate south in winter while others remain north. When and where birds remain

A female eastern bluebird using a sawed-off tree as a perch from which to look for food.

in the North depends on the inclination of individual birds and the local abundance of food.

The typical bluebird breeding habitat is open land with a scattering of trees and low or sparse vegetation. These areas are usually found in suburban or rural locations that have open conservation land, farmland, or orchards.

Even though the eastern bluebird is partially migratory, there are no records of vagrants appearing on the West Coast.

History of Eastern Bluebird Populations

Some of the earliest records of bluebird conservation are in the journals of Henry David Thoreau, who lived in the mid-1800s. He mentions bluebirds revisiting their box, which shows that even then people were putting up nest boxes for birds. From this and other references, it seems that bluebirds were more common in the 1700s and 1800s than they are now.

High populations may have arisen due to the extensive cutting of forests, which created good feeding areas; the planting of apple trees in backyards, which provided good nesting cavities; and the use of wooden fences whose posts eventually also provided cavities for bluebirds.

It is believed that the beginning of the decline in eastern bluebird populations occurred as a result of the introduction of two bird species from Europe — the house sparrow and the starling. The house sparrow was introduced in 1850 and the starling in 1890. Both are aggressive birds that compete successfully with native species for nesting cavities. By 1900 the house sparrow was the most common bird in North America, and by 1940 the starling had spread to almost every part of the United States and southern Canada.

Before the last 50 years, there are few records of bluebird populations. Individual accounts suggest that eastern bluebird populations were probably near their peak around 1900. Then the effects of house sparrow and starling competition and of reductions in open farmland — ideal bluebird habitat — probably began to be felt.

Recent records of eastern bluebird populations show a marked decline from 1938 until the late 1970s. There are now strong indications that eastern bluebird populations are rising and that the birds are repopulating areas where they had not been seen for the last 25 years.

The continual development of nest box trails for bluebirds from the 1970s up to the present has undoubtedly helped to stop the decline and start an increase in bluebird numbers.

Weather also can greatly affect eastern bluebird populations. Cold, freezing rains that cover berries (bluebirds' main winter food) with a layer of ice for a day or two are the most damaging, since this prevents the birds from eating them. Several such ice storms in the last 50 years have had devastating effects, reducing populations in some areas by a third or more. Subsequent data show that the birds can rebound from these losses in the following years, but the recovery is slow.

It is hoped that with the growing awareness of bluebirds' habitat, nesting, and roosting needs, eastern bluebirds can continue to increase in abundance.

A female eastern bluebird and three hungry mouths.

History of Eastern Bluebird Conservation

Many foresighted persons in the 1920s and 1930s could see that the bluebird was going to be crowded out by house sparrows and starlings unless something was done. Two of these people were Thomas E. Musselman and William G. Duncan.

In 1934, Thomas Musselman originated the idea of a "bluebird trail" by placing series of bluebird boxes along roads. He eventually created a trail of more than 1,000 boxes in Adams County, Illinois.

William Duncan set up bluebird trails in Jefferson County, Kentucky, in the 1930s and also designed an excellent basic bluebird nest box (see page 28). Through his education efforts, he is also responsible for thousands of others being involved with helping the bluebirds. The nest box trails and the education of others by Musselman and Duncan mark the real start of bluebird conservation.

This effort at education was picked up and continued on a national basis in 1964 by the formation of the National Association for the Protection and Propagation of the Purple Martin and Bluebirds of America. This group passed on information to members in a monthly newsletter. When the organization disbanded, The Nature Society continued supporting the cause, publishing a regular column on bluebirds in its newspaper, which is now called *The Nature Society News*. For many years this was written by bluebird expert Lawrence Zeleny.

In 1976, Zeleny wrote the book *The Bluebird: How You Can Help Its Fight for Survival,* and this, along with a *National Geographic* article by him on bluebirds, greatly increased public awareness of bluebird conservation needs.

Lawrence Zeleny was instrumental in forming the North American Bluebird Society in 1978; the society has been the continental force in bluebird conservation ever since.

MOUNTAIN BLUEBIRD

Sialia currucoides

Identification

Adult Male Plumage — Sky blue on top of head, back, wings, and tail. Lighter blue from chin to belly and gray-white to white under tail.

Adult Female Plumage — A uniform gray to gray-brown on head, back, throat, breast, and flanks. Sky blue on wings and tail. White on underbelly and under tail. White eye-ring. Just after molting in fall, when feathers are fresh, her chin to flanks are brownish; later, this wears off to a gray-brown.

Juvenal Plumage — Brown to gray on head, back, chin, breast, and along flanks, with lighter spots overlaying breast and flank areas. Conspicuous white eye-ring. This plumage is lost in the mid- to late-summer molt, making juveniles look like adults.

Distinguishing Mountain Bluebirds from Other Bluebirds

Mountain bluebirds are slightly larger than both western and eastern bluebirds. They have longer and thinner bills and their wings are longer, extending to about three-fourths the length of the tail when folded. Mountain bluebirds also tend to hover when hunting, much like an American kestrel. Eastern and western bluebirds hover less.

Male — The male mountain bluebird is easily distinguished from male western and eastern bluebirds by having blue rather than red on the breast.

Female — Distinguished from the eastern and western females by her grayish rather than reddish-brown breast.

A male mountain bluebird perched on a barbed-wire fence.

A male mountain bluebird about to enter his nest box.

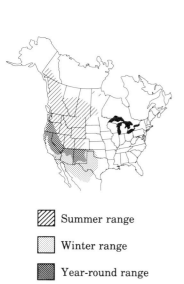

▨ Summer range

☐ Winter range

▩ Year-round range

Hybrids

The mountain bluebird sometimes hybridizes with the eastern bluebird where their ranges overlap. For more on this, see page 15.

The mountain bluebird range broadly overlaps that of the western bluebird, and there are several reports of the two species pairing together and producing hybrid young.

Range and Habitat

The range of the mountain bluebird is hard to fix, for it is continually expanding and contracting. The bird breeds in all the western states and western Canadian provinces, occasionally as far east as northeast North Dakota and as far north as central Alaska. Its winter range extends farther south, into Texas and northern Mexico. The mountain bluebird is undoubtedly able to extend its range into new areas when nest boxes are provided.

Within its range, the mountain bluebird is usually found at higher elevations — above 5,000 feet — and found in meadows and open rangeland. It can also be found in open areas with Douglas fir, limber pine, Jeffrey pine, ponderosa pine, sagebrush, and juniper, and around hayfields and cultivated grainfields.

Since the mountain bluebird is often in habitats where there are few trees, it tends to hover more when feeding. It may be that its longer wings have evolved in relation to this habit.

The mountain bluebird is the most migratory of the three species and, as such, is also the most likely to be found as a vagrant outside its normal range. There have been several reports of mountain bluebirds' showing up in the East in fall and one report in the spring. It has also wandered as far north as Point Barrow, Alaska.

A male mountain bluebird bringing food to nestlings in a natural cavity.

History of Mountain Bluebird Populations

There is very little hard evidence on the status of mountain bluebird populations. Christmas Bird Counts (annual winter censuses in fixed locations) show a steady rise in populations since the early 1960s. This coincides with conservation efforts and the start of massive bluebird trails in the West. Breeding Bird Surveys also show a steady rise in the populations of mountain bluebirds, with most of the increase occurring in western rather than central regions. The North American Bluebird Society's nest box reports also suggest that there are increasing populations of mountain bluebirds along established bluebird trails.

History of Mountain Bluebird Conservation

At the same time that bluebird conservation programs started in the East, people in western states and provinces began to set up trails for mountain bluebirds. The first extensive nest box trail for mountain bluebirds was started by Charles and Winnifred Ellis in 1955 on their farm near Lacombe, Alberta. Their trail was carefully monitored, and house sparrow control was strictly enforced. By the late 1970s, they had the highest nesting density of mountain bluebirds ever recorded. When the Ellis farm was purchased by Union Carbide Canada Ltd. in 1981, a nonprofit company, Ellis Bird Farm Ltd., was established. The mandate of Ellis Bird Farm is to preserve the local mountain bluebird population, support native cavity-nesting bird research and programs, and serve as a center for information on cavity-nesting birds in Alberta.

A female mountain bluebird perched on the new growth of a spruce in spring.

The next large effort to save populations of mountain bluebirds was begun in 1959 by John and Nora Lane of Brandon, Manitoba. They started a boys club, called the Brandon Junior Birders, which built nest boxes and monitored them on roadsides. This, in turn, encouraged others in the region to start their own trails, and pretty soon these trails were joined together to extend 2,500 miles, containing up to 7,000 nest boxes and raising 5,000 bluebirds each year. This was named the Canadian Prairie Bluebird Trail and served mostly mountain bluebirds but some eastern bluebirds as well. Lorne Scott of Indian Head, Saskatchewan, put up and monitored almost 2,000 of these nest boxes all by himself. Stuart and Mary Houston added significantly to the western extension of the trail.

Other important trails have been started by Joy and Cam Finlay in north-central Alberta, Harold Pinel in central Alberta, and Duncan Mackintosh in southern Alberta. He has now helped organize trails of more than 2,500 nest boxes.

In the United States, two pioneering efforts for mountain bluebirds are noteworthy. Trails in Montana have been started by Art Aylesworth and Deni Hershberger. They have also helped distribute educational information on setting up trails and building nest boxes. In addition, there is a trail that now crosses the entire state of Montana from east to west; it houses all three species of bluebirds because it spans such a large area.

In Washington, Jess and Elva Brinkerhoff set up more than 800 nest boxes starting in 1968 and have had tremendous nesting success, with almost all boxes being used. There were few mountain bluebirds in their area before their nest box program was started.

WESTERN BLUEBIRD

Sialia mexicana

Identification

Adult Male Plumage — Deep blue on head, chin, throat, wings, and tail. Back has varying amounts of chestnut mixed in with the blue. Breast and flanks are chestnut; belly and under-tail are gray, wearing down during the year to a blue-gray.

Adult Female Plumage — Head and back are brownish gray; wings and tail are light blue. Throat is light gray, breast and flanks a pale, red-dish brown, and belly and undertail are dull white. She has a dull white eye-ring.

A male western bluebird perched on a mullein seed stalk.

Juvenal Plumage — Brownish gray on head, back, chin, throat, and along flanks. Light flecks on back and light spots on gray-brown breast. Wings and tail blue, with outer tail feathers edged with white. Conspicuous white eye-ring. This plumage is lost in the mid- to late-summer molt, making juveniles look like adults.

Distinguishing Western Bluebirds from Other Bluebirds

Male — Only the male eastern bluebird could be confused with the male western bluebird, since these are the only two bluebirds with red on their breasts. The big difference is that the eastern bluebird has a red breast and chin, whereas the western bluebird has a red breast and a blue chin. The western may also have some red on the back, while the eastern bluebird has an all-blue back.

Female — The female western bluebird is dis-tinguished from the mountain bluebird female by its reddish rather than gray breast and from the female eastern bluebird by its gray rather than reddish-brown chin.

Hybrids

There are several reports of western bluebirds pairing with mountain bluebirds and raising hy-brid young. This is to be expected since their ranges so broadly overlap and they occasionally nest in the same habitat.

Range and Habitat

The western bluebird can be found breeding in most of the western states and British Columbia. It is most abundant along the California coast and in the southwestern states. It winters in

A female western bluebird
in spring.

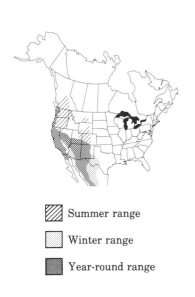

Summer range

Winter range

Year-round range

A female western bluebird on a favorite perch.

many of the same areas, for it is not strongly migratory. Instead, it just moves to lower elevations and wanders about in search of areas with abundant food. It is also known to move into some of the more desertlike areas of the Southwest during winter.

The western bluebird breeds in open farmland, orchards, at forest edges, and in open conifer or broadleaf woodlands.

There are no vagrants reported for this species, probably because it has so little tendency to migrate.

History of Western Bluebird Populations

Western bluebird populations have been best studied in the Northwest. When the first white settlers moved into this area in the 1880s, they probably increased the amount of good western bluebird habitat by clearing forests and creating farmland. Thus, early farmers may have seen an increase in western bluebirds in the first decades after settling.

In the early 1900s, western bluebirds started to decrease in number in the Northwest until, by the mid-1940s, they were almost extinct along the coasts of Oregon, Washington, and the southern half of Vancouver Island.

There have been many theories as to why the bluebird population fell so rapidly in these areas. Certainly the house sparrow was one factor, taking over many of the nesting spots of the bluebirds. In addition, house sparrows took over the city nesting spots of violet-green and tree swallows, forcing them into the countryside, where they too competed with western bluebirds for nesting cavities.

The starling was probably not an initial factor in the western bluebird's decline, since bluebird populations were dropping way before the starling became established in the northwest region, which was not until the 1960s.

In addition to competition from the house sparrow, changing agricultural practices reduced the amount of good bluebird habitat. Hydroelectric dams were constructed, providing cheap means for irrigating crops, and large portable sprinklers were widely used. Both of these led to large-scale

A male western bluebird pausing from his daily activities.

farming of more valuable crops. This, in turn, led to the conversion of old, small farms into huge agricultural areas. The old farmland, with its interspersed clearings and woodlands, was the better bluebird habitat. Also, tractor-driven plows could go right up to the fence line, eliminating hedgerows that were good for nesting and for the production of winter berries on which bluebirds could feed.

In the 1970s, bluebird trails were begun, and now the western bluebird is beginning to make a comeback in certain parts of the Northwest. Still, more work needs to be done. Since there have been few population studies in many other parts of its range, we have little knowledge of how the western bluebird is doing in general.

Christmas Bird Counts show a modest increase and Breeding Bird Surveys show either steady or slightly rising populations of western bluebirds in the last 15 years, at least on a nationwide basis. But we need to have even more extensive records made of this lovely bird throughout its range, in order to be sure that these studies are an accurate reflection of western bluebird populations as a whole.

History of Western Bluebird Conservation

Hubert Prescott of Portland, Oregon, was one of the first people to take steps toward rebuilding the populations of the western bluebird in the Northwest. With a great deal of study and care, he started three different nest box trails in his area of the state in 1971. Western bluebirds are now successfully breeding where they had not been seen for decades, and this effort has inspired other, similar trails in the Northwest. The Audubon Society of Corvallis Bluebird Trail has provided the most comprehensive base study of bluebirds in Oregon. Detailed nest box records and banding reports have been contributed by volunteers since 1976.

There is still a great deal more that needs to be done for the western bluebird.

BLUEBIRD NEST BOXES

Talk About Boxes

Bluebirds are called secondary cavity nesters, which means that they are unable to create the kind of nest cavities they need but must rely on what is already available in an area. It is a simple equation: no nesting cavities equals no bluebirds. Unfortunately, the number of natural nest sites available to bluebirds is on the decline. That is where nest boxes come in.

It is probably safe to say that there are as many theories about bluebird nest box design as there are people putting up nest boxes. Bluebirders can talk for hours on the subject, and once you start putting up your own nest boxes, you are sure to have your own ideas as well. The discussion has its enjoyable aspects, for there is always room for experimentation and improvements and, when it comes right down to it, the birds will accept a wide variety of boxes and nesting situations.

Having said this, we hasten to add that a great deal has been learned about bluebird nest boxes over the last 50 years and that when buying or building a bluebird nest box you should be aware of certain key points. These are summarized in the checklist in this chapter, and the areas needing further elaboration are covered below. For where to put a box, see page 39.

What Size Entrance Hole?
What Size Box?

The traditional size entrance hole for all bluebird boxes has been 1½ inches in diameter. This size enables bluebirds to enter but keeps the larger starlings from getting in and taking over. This is important, since starlings are aggressive cavity nesters and often take over nesting spots of many other species, especially the bluebird.

Recently, as more emphasis has been placed on attracting mountain and western bluebirds, it has been discovered that at least some mountain bluebirds have trouble entering the 1½-inch-diameter hole. After some experimenting (for which, again, bluebirders have a penchant), it was found that mountain bluebirds prefer slightly larger entrance holes. An entrance hole of 1⁹⁄₁₆ inches in diameter was found to be the perfect size, for it admits the bluebirds but still excludes starlings.

Now it is recommended that you use this larger size entrance hole for mountain *and* western bluebirds, since in many cases their ranges overlap and you may not be sure which species you will attract.

The other important dimension is the floor area inside the box. Again, traditionally, a good bluebird nest box had a floor area of 4 by 4 inches or 4½ by 4½ inches. But the mountain and western bluebirds average larger clutches than the eastern bluebird, up to a maximum of 8 eggs. Because of this, it has been recommended that the interior floor dimensions of their nest boxes be 5–5½ inches on a side. Many people have found that eastern bluebirds accept these larger boxes as well.

In winter, when several birds may roost in one box at a time, the larger floor area, in addition, may make it safer for all three species by preventing overcrowding.

Materials, Finishes, Insulation, and Ventilation

Another of the questions often asked about bluebird boxes is: What material should they be made of? There are many choices these days, including plastic, ceramic, wood, metal, and a mixture of concrete and sawdust.

10 Features of a Successful Bluebird Box: A Checklist

Whether you buy or make a bluebird nest box, be sure that it meets these criteria.

1. **No perch** should be attached to the front of the box, for this may encourage house sparrows, which are undesirable competitors.

2. **Entrance holes** should be 1½ inches in diameter for eastern bluebirds and 1⁹⁄₁₆ inches for mountain and western bluebirds. If the hole is oval, it should be 1⅜ inches wide and 2¼ inches long.

3. **Floor dimensions** should be approximately 4 by 4 inches for eastern bluebirds and 5 by 5 inches for mountain and western bluebirds.

4. **Height** from top of floor to bottom of entrance hole should be approximately 5–7 inches.

5. **Opening the box** should be easy for monitoring and cleaning. Side- or front-opening boxes are easiest to clean, but top-opening boxes are easiest to monitor.

6. **Ventilation** by means of small holes drilled at the top of the sides or back, or gaps left between the roof and sides or front, should be provided.

7. **Drainage holes,** such as holes drilled in the floor or space between the floor and the sides, should be present.

8. **Attaching the box** to a tree or post should be easy. Be sure this has been provided for.

9. **At least ¾-inch-thick wood** should be used as the building material to provide adequate insulation from the sun.

10. **The roof should overhang** the entrance hole by at least 1–2 inches to keep out rain and shade the entrance.

Besides food, all this male eastern bluebird needs is a good nest box in which to breed.

Wood is still probably the safest and best all-around material with which to make bluebird nest boxes. This is because wood mimics natural nest cavities, is relatively inexpensive, is easy to work with, and provides good insulation. Pine, cedar, and exterior plywood are all good choices.

Wood preservatives are another issue. It is generally agreed that pressure-treated lumber should not be used, because of the chemicals in it. Finishes and stains should be applied only to the outside of the box and should not be too dark, since dark colors absorb more heat and will make the box hotter. Linseed oil is a good, safe preservative and stain, but be sure it is thoroughly dry before setting the box out.

Some nest boxes can overheat in summer. Birdhouses that sit out in the sun develop inside temperatures higher than those of the air outside the house. In some birdhouses, the internal temperature can be as much as 22°F higher than the outside air temperature. Any box that reaches an inside temperature of over 107°F could harm the eggs or nestlings. It is important that this not occur in your nest boxes.

Three factors in the construction of a birdhouse that affect its internal temperature are materials, color, and ventilation.

Of the various materials used for birdhouses — wood, ceramics, plastic, metal, mixed concrete and sawdust — wood is the best insulator from heat. But the thickness of the wood matters. Most general lumber that is called 1 inch thick actually measures ¾ inch thick, and this is fine for birdhouses. Lumber or plywood thinner than this will not provide equally good insulation and will create a warmer temperature inside the house. This is especially important in hotter climates.

The next issue is color. Light-colored birdhouses are cooler than dark ones. And it is not just the top that has to be lighter, but the sides as well. Natural wood color works well and does not keep the birds from using the house as some bright, light color might. Birdhouses painted dark green or stained dark brown will be substantially hotter inside.

To help protect from overheating, all nest boxes should also have ventilation other than just the entrance hole. This should consist of ¼-inch to ½-inch holes drilled in the top of the sides of the box or a space between the top of the box and the sides. This kind of ventilation can reduce the inside temperature of the box considerably.

If you live in an area where summer temperatures are regularly over 90°F, then you should create a ½-inch gap between the top of each side and the roof for cross ventilation. You may also want to place your birdhouses in at least partial shade.

Opening the Nest Box

All bluebird nest boxes should be monitored during the nesting season (see Monitoring Bluebird Boxes, page 42). In order to do this effectively, you need an easy way to open the box and look inside. There are three ways to open a nest box: from the top, from the front, and from the side.

Top-opening boxes generally have the roof hinged at the back so that it can be lifted up (see the photograph on page 43). These can be good, for they may be the least disturbing to the birds.

However, they do not enable you to clean out the box by getting underneath the nest. They also do not enable you to easily look for nest parasites, such as blowflies. To look into a top-opening box, you must either be fairly tall or mount the box low, which may make it more susceptible to predators.

In front-opening boxes the front panel generally is attached at the top and opens out and up from the bottom (see the photograph on page 45). These enable you to look directly into and underneath the nest at the same time. They also make it easy to clean out the old nest when breeding is over. However, if any extension is added to the entrance hole as protection against predators, then it may be difficult to open the front all the way, since the extension may bump into the roof overhang.

Side-opening boxes, in which a side panel swings out and up from the bottom, are similar to the front-opening boxes, with the additional advantage that the overhanging roof does not interfere with lifting up the side.

Types of Nest Boxes

Several designs of bluebird boxes have become well known over the years and are used by a great number of bluebirders. Among these are the Peterson Bluebird House and the Duncan Bluebird House. Each of these boxes offers certain advantages.

The Duncan Bluebird House was developed about 50 years ago by William G. Duncan. It is an excellent standard box that any bluebird would be happy to use. It has a generous floor area 4½ by 5 inches, drainage holes in the corners of the floor, and ventilation at the tops of the sides, and it is side opening. It is also fairly easy to make and put up.

The Peterson Bluebird House is more complex in its design. It was originated by Dick Peterson over 30 years ago and has acquired many avid supporters since. Its sloping roof and front help keep rain from getting in; the front opens from the top down, making it easy to look in; 2-by-4's are used for the front and back and provide added insulation from heat; the small area of the floor at the bottom requires the gathering of less nest-

Several standard boxes that can be bought. Clockwise from lower left corner: Peterson Bluebird House, Duncan Bluebird House, and then four nest boxes available through the North American Bluebird Society.

building material by the birds, but the box still has plenty of room for large clutches; and the oval entrance hole is designed to make it easier for the adults to go in and out.

These nest boxes just happen to be known by name. There are many other excellent nest boxes produced for bluebirds, and you should not hesitate to use them. The North American Bluebird Society offers several, as do other bluebird organizations and retailers. See Resources, page 95.

Roost Boxes

Although bluebirds are territorial in summer, they are not territorial in winter and, in fact, may roost together in the same box. In recent years, there has been more study of bluebird roosting habits (see pages 90–91). It is clear from these studies that many nest boxes are used as roost boxes in winter.

In the past, specific roost box designs have been suggested. These were generally tall boxes with an entrance hole at the bottom of the box front and separate perches near the top inside. The theory behind this design is that heat rises and gets trapped in the top of the box where the birds will perch. However, roosting bluebirds go to the base of a cavity and huddle together for added warmth. In this roosting box they would thus tend to stay at the bottom, where it is colder, and would block the entrance for other bluebirds, meaning there would be less group warmth. Because of this, normal nest boxes are better roosting sites for bluebirds than this type of roosting box.

Normal nest boxes can be improved as roost boxes if they are insulated against drafts. Their ventilation holes and drainage holes can be plugged with soft material such as felt or weather stripping. This can be put in place in the fall and then taken out in the spring before the birds start nesting again.

Plans for a Bluebird Nest Box

Making a bluebird nest box can be a wonderful project for any member of the family, or it can be done by school, church, or scout groups. It is also an excellent way to foster interest in birds and the environment.

We have included our own plans for an easily made bluebird nest box. There is nothing wildly unique about it. It just has all of the requisites of an excellent bluebird nest box and is also easy to build.

Directions — The whole box can be built from lumber 1 inch by 6 inches (which actually measures ¾ inch by 5½ inches) by 5 feet long. Pine or cedar boards are good choices. In areas where pine or cedar is not available, ¾-inch plywood can be used.

1. Draw the various pieces to size on the board and cut them out. This can be done with either a hand saw or an electric saw.

2. In the front panel, drill the entrance hole 1½ inches in diameter for eastern bluebirds and 1⁹⁄₁₆ inches for mountain and western bluebirds. Then drill ¼-inch-diameter ventilation holes near the top of each side piece. Next drill a ⅛-inch-diameter hole near the bottom of the right-hand side, where it will overlap the floor; a fastener will go through it and screw into the edge of the floor to keep the side-opening door closed. Finally, drill holes near the top and bottom of the back panel for mounting the box.

3. Nail the pieces together with galvanized nails. Be sure to fasten the right-hand side panel near the top only — one nail through the front of the box and one nail through the back — placing each nail 8 inches up from the bottom. This will allow the side to pivot open on these nails.

4. A small strip of wood can be nailed to cover the seam where the top meets the back, in order to keep rain out.

5. The outside of the box can be finished with a little linseed oil. Let it be totally absorbed and dry before putting up the box.

6. Be sure the side opens smoothly, and then place a fastener, such as a screw eye, through the hole drilled for that purpose and into the floor to hold it closed.

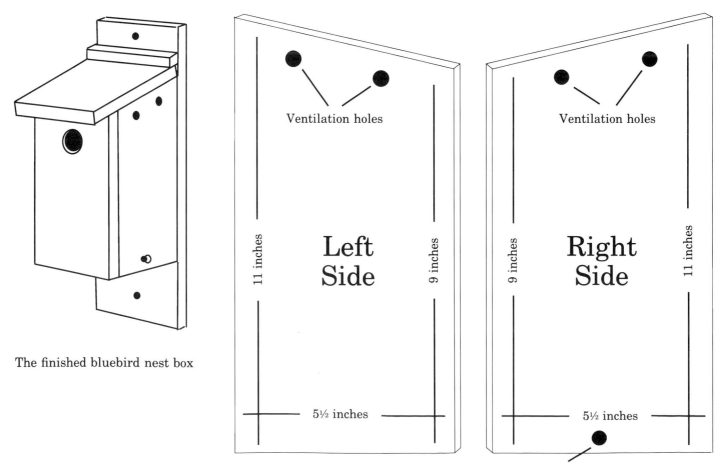

The finished bluebird nest box

Ventilation holes

11 inches

Left Side

9 inches

5½ inches

9 inches

Right Side

11 inches

Ventilation holes

5½ inches

Hole for fastener

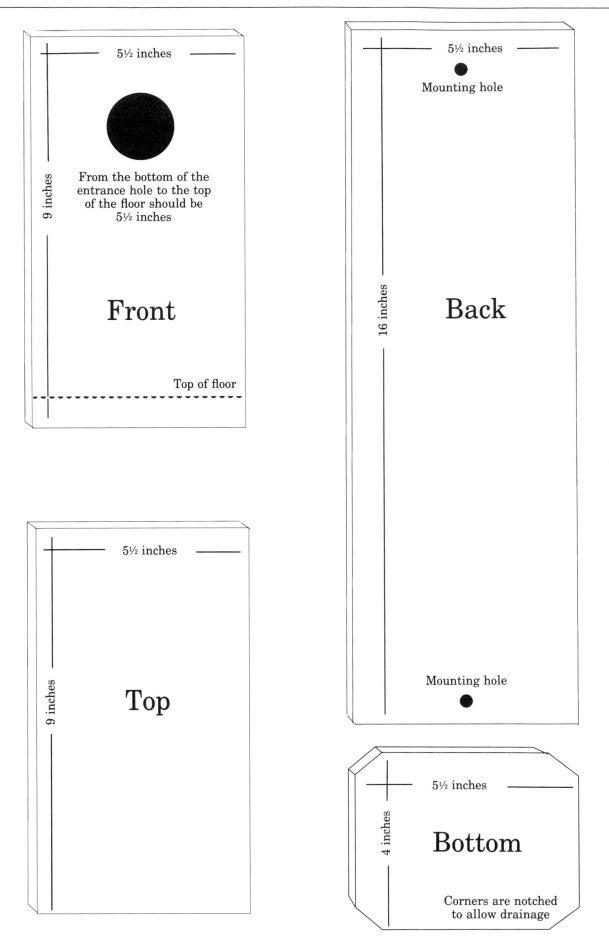

5½ inches

From the bottom of the
entrance hole to the top
of the floor should be
5½ inches

Front

9 inches

Top of floor

5½ inches

Mounting hole

Back

16 inches

Mounting hole

5½ inches

Top

9 inches

5½ inches

Bottom

4 inches

Corners are notched
to allow drainage

LANDSCAPING FOR BLUEBIRDS

Attracting Bluebirds to Your Yard

There are many things that you can do to make a suburban or rural yard more attractive to bluebirds, both in summer and in winter (providing the birds winter in your area). Bluebirds' needs change over the year, and by understanding these needs and changes you can improve your backyard habitat and have a greater chance of drawing these beautiful birds to it.

A female eastern bluebird hovering as she eats the berries from pokeweed.

Summer Needs of Bluebirds

In summer, bluebirds need nesting cavities, foraging perches, and areas of low or sparse vegetation that contain an abundance of insects.

In spring, summer, and fall, bluebirds eat primarily insects. They usually sit on perches and look for insects on the ground, then quickly dive down to get the insect and return to the perch. When there are no perches to hunt from, they may hover over the ground as they look for insects and then drop down when they spot one. Hovering is more common among mountain bluebirds than among western or eastern bluebirds.

Bluebirds' favorite foods include grasshoppers, crickets, ground beetles, and caterpillars. They also love spiders found among the grasses. Bluebirds prefer to hunt for insects in either sparse or low-cut vegetation because in these habitats the insects are more easily seen.

In addition to insects, bluebirds will feed on berries that ripen in summer. A list of these is included in the chart in this chapter.

Bluebirds need perches for many activities including advertising territory, surveying the area for intruders and predators, and interacting with their mate. But most important, they use them as places from which to look for food on the ground below.

Attracting Bluebirds in Summer

Keep Vegetation Low — Since low-cut or sparse vegetation is optimal habitat for bluebird foraging, you should keep some areas of fields cut low. If you have areas with sparse vegetation, leave them as they are; otherwise, take out or prune shrubbery so that the bluebirds can see and get to the ground easily.

A male eastern bluebird on a perch with a spider that it just picked up from the ground.

We have a large field in which the grasses tend to grow 3–4 feet tall. We mow it several times during the summer in order to keep it a better feeding site for the bluebirds. Instead of trying to make this mowed area a lawn with only grasses, we let a variety of weeds and plants grow in it, since this creates a more natural environment for insects on which the bluebirds and other birds can feed.

Create Good Perches — Open perches are essential for a good bluebird summer habitat. Bluebirds generally feed in about a 20-foot radius from a perch. Thus, if perches are scattered about an area, the bluebirds will be more able to utilize all the existing food.

To create good perches, keep trees pruned to at least 10 feet above the ground and clear some of the lower limbs of leaves. If you have any dead limbs or dead trees that are no danger to people, leave them as perches for the birds.

If you have an excellent feeding area for bluebirds, but no perches, then you can make your own. We have had success using tomato stakes, each with a small crossbar nailed on top. We pound several stakes into open areas of the bluebird's territory where there are no perches. Within minutes, the birds begin using them as foraging spots. Some people have had success with cutting down small dead trees 10–12 feet tall and sticking them in the ground in bluebird areas.

These perches make good lookouts, and they provide safe spots for resting; the birds often fly from one to another as they move about. We find that stakes of the same type placed in our garden are used by swallows, hummingbirds, cardinals, mockingbirds, song sparrows, and many other species.

Preserve Potential Sites for Natural Cavities — Until recently, dead, broken limbs remaining on trees — called snags — were considered a nuisance and an eyesore by foresters and landscapers, who recommended that they be removed from living trees whenever possible. What was not appreciated at the time was the value of snags to many forms of wildlife, especially cavity-nesting birds. With the growth of environmental awareness in recent decades, the retention of snags on trees has come to be seen as a positive step people can take to promote wildlife on their own properties.

This is particularly true in landscaping for bluebirds. Bluebirds use snags as places from which to look for food and defend territory, and as places where they can groom, mate, seek safety, and rest. Snags also become an important source of natural cavities for bluebirds, since many woodpeckers and other so-called primary cavity nesters excavate holes in them.

Here are some tips for saving snags and dead trees: First, preserve snags and dead trees within 15 yards of clearings, for these are most likely to be used by bluebirds as perches, or if they have natural cavities, as nest or roost sites. Second, keep dead trees and snags spaced out over an area. Third, if a tree looks as if some of its limbs are diseased or dying, leave them alone, for these limbs may become good snags.

We have a beautiful old ash tree at the edge of our field, and although we are sorry to see it slowly dying back, we know that in its old age it will provide numerous valuable cavity sites and perches for bluebirds as well as other bird species.

Berry-Producing Plants That Attract Bluebirds

For Summer or Autumn Fruits

Trees
American Holly, *Ilex opaca*
Black Cherry, *Prunus serotina*
Cascara Buckthorn, *Rhamnus purshiana*
Crabapples, *Malus* spp.
European Mountain Ash, *Sorbus aucuparia*
Kousa Dogwood, *Cornus kousa*
Pin Cherry, *Prunus pennsylvanica*
Red Mulberry, *Morus rubra*
White Mulberry, *Morus alba*

Shrubs
Autumn Olive, *Elaeagnus umbellata*
Blackberry, Raspberry, *Rubus* spp.
Blueberry, *Vaccinium* spp.
Chokeberry, *Aronia* spp.
Chokecherry, *Prunus virginiana*
Dogwood shrubs, *Cornus* spp.
Elderberry, *Sambucus* spp.
Honeysuckle, *Lonicera* spp.
Russian Olive, *Elaeagnus angustifolia*
Shadbush, *Amelanchier* spp.
Snowberry, *Symphoricarpos albus*
Viburnams, *Viburnam* spp.

Vines
Grape, *Vitis* spp.
Greenbriar, *Smilax* spp.
Honeysuckle, *Lonicera* spp.

Herbaceous Plants
Pokeweed, *Phytolocca americana*

For Winter Fruits

Trees
Flowering Dogwood, *Cornus florida*
Hackberry, *Celtis occidentalis*
Hawthorns, *Crataegus* spp.
Madrone, *Arbutus menziesii*
Mountain Ash, *Sorbus americana*
Red Cedar, *Juniperus virginianum*
Sour Gum, *Nyssa sylvatica*
Western Red Cedar, *Juniperus scopulorum*

Shrubs
Bayberry, *Myrica carolinensis*
Blackhaw, *Viburnam prunifolium*
Cotoneaster, *Cotoneaster* spp.
Highbush Cranberry, *Viburnum trilobum*
Holly, *Ilex* spp.
Mistletoe, *Phoradendron* spp.
Multiflora Rose, *Rosa multiflora*
Sumac, *Rhus* spp.

Vines
Bittersweet, *Celastrus* spp.
Japanese Honeysuckle, *Lonicera japonica*
Moonseed, *Menispermum canadense*
Pyracantha, *Pyracantha* spp.
Virginia Creeper, *Parthenocissus quinque-folia*

A male mountain bluebird taking a drink at a birdbath.

Provide Water — Bluebirds are often very attracted to water. Even just a small birdbath placed where the birds can easily see it and get to it safely can attract many bluebirds. The water should be about 1–1½ inches deep. Keep the bath in an open area so the birds can watch for predators, and provide a perch nearby where they can go before or after using the bath.

Water, in fact, is not just a summer attraction. There is one account of western bluebirds in Oregon using a birdbath every day in winter — as many as 8 bluebirds at one time. They often bathed in the late afternoon, then carefully preened themselves before going into roost boxes for the night.

Winter Needs of Bluebirds

Bluebirds do not have fixed migration routes or wintering areas to which they always return. Instead they are more flexible and can overwinter just about anywhere, as long as they have food, water, shelter during the day, and places to roost at night.

The main winter foods of bluebirds are not insects as in summer, but berries from shrubs, vines, and trees. (This is especially so in areas where temperatures are regularly below freezing and thus inhibit all insect activity.) If you can provide these natural sources of food for the birds,

they may stay on your property longer in fall and possibly even through winter. These plants can also provide some shelter during the day.

Attracting Bluebirds in Winter

Plant Shrubs with Berries — When you are considering which berry-producing plants to use, there are several points to keep in mind. For winter food, be sure to have plants whose berries ripen in late fall, rather than in summer, for summer berries are usually eaten before winter. Select plants that grow well in your area of the country and your planting zone. Choose plants that produce lots of berries and berries that have a large proportion of fruit to seed, for the birds eat the whole berry, then pass on the seeds in their droppings and retain only the fruit portion for nutrition.

Of course, berries can be attractive to bluebirds at any time of year. So our list of berry-producing plants (on the facing page) includes both those that fruit in summer and fall and those that fruit in winter.

Additional Winter Measures — In addition to having berry plants, you can offer water, food in various kinds of feeders, and boxes for roosting. See page 29, page 36, and page 88.

BLUEBIRD FEEDERS

Bluebirds at Feeders

Even though there are reports of their coming to feeders and eating raisins, fruits, suet, and hulled sunflower seeds, bluebirds are not generally considered feeder birds, for their main food is berries or insects and not seeds.

However, in recent years there have been more frequent attempts to design feeders specifically for bluebirds. Much experimentation has gone on, but there is still lots of room for bluebirders to develop new feeder designs and try new foods. We

A bluebird feeder with a suet mixture and 9 bluebirds.

encourage you to experiment and see which feeder designs and what kinds of food work for your bluebirds.

Types of Feeders

A bluebird feeder can be as simple as a plastic coffee-can lid filled with mealworms or raisins and nailed on top of a stake or to the roof of a bluebird box. Bluebirds also have been attracted to logs with holes drilled in them and filled with suet or a suet-type mixture (see the recipe later in this chapter). The logs can be hung vertically or placed horizontally.

There are several other feeder designs that bluebirders have tried. The common denominator to these is a roofed box with entry holes in the sides; the food is placed inside. For the eastern bluebird the holes are 1½ inches in diameter; for the western and mountain bluebird they are 1⁹/₁₆ inches in diameter. This size entry hole helps exclude potential competitors, such as starlings or mockingbirds. Many of these feeders have two entry holes, making it easier for several bluebirds to feed at once.

The feeder box can be all wood, or two sides may be Plexiglas, enabling the birds to see the food. Mark lines on the clear sides with magic marker or tape so the birds can tell that it is not a way in or out of the feeder. Some people put the food in a removable tray for ease of filling and cleaning. Use a small glass custard cup for mealworms; it contains the mealworms and makes them visible to bluebirds.

Mount the feeder on a sturdy post or pole out in the open and near where bluebirds perch or are frequently seen. Put a predator guard on the pole to prevent raccoons from reaching the feeder (see Protection from Predators, page 50).

This bluebird feeder has the important elements: properly sized entrance holes and clear sides to help the birds see the food. Lines can be drawn on the clear sides to show that they are not a way in or out of the feeder.

Kinds of Food

For food, try small pieces of suet, currants, sunflower hearts, mealworms (sold in pet stores), or berries such as those of dogwood, multiflora rose, or sumac. Raisins, especially those that have been softened by soaking briefly in boiling water, are appealing to bluebirds. Another option is to make your own suet mixture.

Here is a basic recipe that you can adapt by adding your own ingredients:

½ cup peanut butter
½ cup solid vegetable shortening or lard
2 cups cornmeal
1 cup flour
chopped raisins, nut meats, or peanut hearts

Only use peanut butter in a mixture; used alone, it may stick in the birds' crop. We mix this in the food processor until it is the consistency of putty and then store any extra in the refrigerator.

Training Bluebirds to Use the Feeder

How soon bluebirds recognize and learn to use a feeder varies considerably. Some birds enter the feeder as soon as it is put out. Others need more help learning to enter a hole to get the food. Some bluebirders recommend starting with just a feeding platform, getting the birds used to that, and then adding a roof and one side at a time. Others have gotten bluebirds interested in a feeder by attaching sprigs of berries to the outside of the feeder, on the roof or on a tray near the entrance hole. Stakes with crossbars nailed to the top can be put several feet away from the feeder and serve as perches for birds that are coming and going.

Mockingbirds may chase bluebirds from feeders, especially if the food is on a tray and the mockingbird can get it. Move feeders outside mockingbirds' territory, which is usually about 1–2 acres.

When to Use Feeders

One of the best things about bluebird feeders is that they can help the birds get through temporary shortages of food caused by unfavorable weather early in the breeding season. They can be a big help to an incubating female who might have to desert her eggs if the weather is cold and insects and berries are scarce. Feeders can also help bluebirds in the nestling and fledgling stages, when the demands for food are great. It has been suggested that feeders not be used in late fall in the North, where they might keep bluebirds from migrating. On the other hand, in northern areas where bluebirds are known to be overwintering, feeders may significantly help the birds to survive certain storms and cold spells.

SETTING UP A BLUEBIRD BOX OR TRAIL

What Is a Bluebird Trail?

A bluebird trail is a series of nest boxes spaced about 300 feet apart. Trails can consist of just a few boxes in a large backyard to hundreds or even thousands of boxes put up over large areas of countryside. Thomas E. Musselman came up with the idea; he placed bluebird nest boxes along stretches of road.

It is important to realize that you do not have to have a bluebird trail in order to attract bluebirds. Just a single nest box appropriately placed can attract the birds. On the other hand, if you have the space and resources for a trail, you may help more bluebirds nest successfully.

A U-post mounting pole with nest box attached.

Poles for Mounting Boxes

After either buying or making bluebird nest boxes, your next activity will be mounting them. Boxes can be mounted on poles, fence posts, utility poles, and trees.

Posts or poles are the best for providing protection from predators, for you can easily add various kinds of predator guards to them. There are basically three types of posts that you may use: wooden posts, garden U-posts, and metal pipes. Wooden posts can be hardwood garden stakes that are ¾ inch square and about 6 feet long. These are a bit fragile and will not last as long as a 2-by-2-inch or 2-by-3-inch board, which is also inexpensive. Nest boxes can be attached with screws, wire, or bolts.

Better than either of these is what is called a U-post. It is a green metal post shaped in cross section like a U. Each post usually has several evenly spaced holes and little projecting hooks on which wire fencing is placed. Partway up the base of the post is a flat fin that keeps the post from swaying after it is rammed into the ground. You can buy 5- to 6-foot lengths that are lightweight or 6- to 7-foot lengths that are heavyweight. Both can be bought at hardware or garden stores, or sometimes lumber yards. Nest boxes can be attached to them with bolts or wire.

Posts made of metal pipe are also good, but the piping is not as easy to buy and is heavier to work with. Some people put a shorter-length pipe with a slightly wider diameter into the ground and then put the mounting pipe into that for greater stability.

An alternative to buying poles or posts is to use existing fence posts or utility poles. In either case, you must have the permission of the owner before doing so. When using fence posts, place the boxes outside areas where livestock may rub

This wonderful rural setting would be perfect for a bluebird nest box or trail.

against them to scratch. When possible, face boxes toward the next fence post so that the birds can look into the entrance from a perch.

You need permission from the utility company before mounting nest boxes on their poles. This is not always easy to get. Another potential problem is that utility poles offer some species of hawks a perch above the nest; this can be hazardous to the bluebirds, who might be caught as they leave the box.

Bluebird nest boxes can be mounted on trees, but this is one of the least desirable alternatives. Trees invite climbing predators; it is hard to protect nest boxes on trees from cats, raccoons, snakes, and squirrels. A tree-mounted nest box may attract competitors such as house wrens, who can also be predators at times.

What Height / What Direction / What Time of Year

The bottom of the bluebird box should be at least 3 feet above the ground. A box mounted 4–5 feet high is ideal. The birds are flexible and may nest up to 15 feet in the air or higher. Your main considerations in box height should be deterring climbing predators and allowing easy monitoring.

There is no one compass direction that bluebirds favor over another. However, you can aid the bluebirds by facing the box away from prevailing winds and, in hot climates, placing it to face north or east to avoid direct midday and afternoon sun. Perhaps more important is facing the box toward some tree, shrub, or fence post within 100 feet, for when the nestlings leave the

A fine location for a nest box or trail in the West. This box belongs to a pair of western bluebirds in Montana.

nest they make an initial flight to safety, and this will offer them an easy mark.

When should you put up nest boxes? As soon as possible. Bluebirds start looking for breeding nest boxes by February in the South and by March in the North. And where bluebirds have three broods, they can use them for breeding well into August. In fall, bluebirds often explore boxes briefly as they move about feeding, and in winter they can use boxes for roosting at night. Thus, at any time of year, bluebirds are interacting with nest boxes.

Think Habitat First

The most important factor in attracting nesting bluebirds is to place the boxes in good bluebird habitat. Even the best nest box will not attract bluebirds if it is in the wrong place.

Listed below are some aspects of a good bluebird habitat that apply to all three species.

1. Bluebirds nest primarily in suburban and rural areas.

2. During breeding, bluebirds hunt insects by scanning the ground from a perch, spotting the insect, and then dropping down to the ground to get it. Scattered young trees or shrubs, fence posts, and the lower branches of a lone mature tree make good hunting perches. Fences are ideal since they provide continuous perching spots in open areas. Four- to five-foot stakes driven into the ground 10–20 yards from a nest box are readily used by bluebirds.

3. Sparse or low vegetation is also important, since it enables the bluebirds to see and capture the insects. Cut meadows, mowed lawns, and grazed fields are all good bluebird habitat.

4. Nest boxes should be at least 100 feet from brushy or wooded areas where wrens are likely to be and, preferably, at least a quarter of a mile or more from farmyards and barns where house sparrows live.

5. Good areas for bluebird nest boxes include: open fields, fence rows, orchards where there is no pesticide spraying, cemeteries, large lawns, golf courses, public parks, along open highways that are kept mowed, and pastureland.

In addition to these habitats, the mountain bluebird also nests in open conifer woodlands, and in cliffs or clay banks along rivers.

If you do not have a good bluebird habitat on your property, consider putting up a trail on some other appropriate area in your town or community. Always secure permission from the landowner before placing any bluebird boxes on land that you do not own.

Spacing

Bluebirds are territorial when breeding and have territories of about 2–3 acres. Over the years it has been found that they do not generally nest closer than about 100 yards from the next bluebird, although there have been exceptions to this. Therefore, bluebird trails usually space nest boxes this distance apart.

In areas where swallows compete with bluebirds for nest sites, boxes can be paired 5–15 feet

An example of a suburban habitat where eastern bluebirds are nesting. Both boxes are 10 feet from a road. Bluebirds are living in box on right, swallows in box on left. The white PVC pipe below the bluebird box protects it from raccoons, which are prevalent in suburban areas.

apart. Swallows will nest in only one, leaving the other open for bluebirds. For more on this, see pages 47–48.

Vandalism

In some cases, nest boxes are vandalized by humans. It is hard for us to understand why anyone would do this, but it does occur. Nest boxes can be shot at and torn down.

There are several ways to minimize the chances of this occurring. One is to place your nest boxes in out-of-the-way places where they do not attract people's attention. Another is to put a small sign on the box or simply write on it something to the effect that this is an official bluebird nest box and that disturbing it is against the law, which is true.

Another option is to work with the community and educate your neighbors about the nest boxes. Write a small article for your local newspaper about bluebirds and bluebird nest boxes, or have a community group help build and put up the boxes. An educated public will be a more concerned and respectful public.

MONITORING BLUEBIRD BOXES

What Is Monitoring?

It is not enough just to put up bluebird boxes. To attract bluebirds successfully the boxes must be monitored, or checked, at least once a week. The function of monitoring is to keep house sparrows from using bluebird boxes, to check on the general health and safety of the bluebirds, and to allow detailed record keeping of their progress.

A male eastern bluebird at a nest hole formerly excavated by a hairy woodpecker in the trunk of a white birch tree. The nests in the wild have to make it on their own, without our monitoring.

How to Monitor

To monitor a nest box, go quickly and quietly to the box, open it, and look inside. We tap on the box first or speak softly, just in case an adult bird is inside, so that it has a chance to leave. Usually the bird flies out at our approach, but sometimes an incubating female remains calmly on the nest when we open the box. In that case, we leave her undisturbed and come back at another time.

Do not worry that your presence will make the parents desert the nest. Bluebirds are very tolerant of human presence. It is also *not* true that if you touch the nest your scent will make the birds leave. Most birds have a very poorly developed sense of smell.

We have monitored nest boxes as frequently as once a day without any harm to the birds, but we would not recommend doing it any more often than this.

When Not to Monitor the Nest

The only time you should not monitor is when the nestlings are 12 days old or older in the case of the eastern bluebird, or 14 days old or older in the case of the mountain and western bluebird. The reason for this is that they may bolt from the nest prematurely at that age. They will not be able to fly nor be as capable of surviving in the wild as they would if they had stayed in the box until the time they would normally fledge.

You might think that you could place nestlings that flew out of the box back inside, but this does not work. They are likely to jump out again. Once out of the nest, the young do not return.

To identify when the young are just about 12 days old, you must have followed their progress previously and kept records of when they hatched. You may also be able to estimate their

A male eastern bluebird at the nest box entrance while the female waits above with food for the nestlings.

age by using the pictures and guides in the chapter on nestlings, page 80. When in doubt, don't open the box; just observe it from a distance.

If you accidentally cause the young to prematurely fledge, replace them in the box and place a hole restrictor — a false front with a 1⅛-inch-diameter opening — on the box. This will prevent the young from leaving, but the parents will still be able to feed them. Quietly remove the hole restrictor that night after dark.

Remove House Sparrow Nests

If you want bluebirds, you must not let house sparrows establish themselves in your nest boxes. House sparrows are aggressive competitors for bluebird houses and will even kill bluebirds and take over their boxes. Remove any house sparrow nests that you find. Study the picture of the nests shown in Dealing with Competitors (page 48) and learn to recognize a house sparrow nest. House sparrow nests are always sloppier than bluebird or swallow nests and contain grass strands and other fibers haphazardly spread all over inside the box. Of course, the best clue is seeing the house sparrow using the box.

Do not remove the nests of any other nesting birds, such as chickadees, titmice, tree and violet-green swallows, or wrens. These birds are all protected by federal law, but house sparrows, starlings, and pigeons are not.

Record What You See

One of the joys of bluebirding is to watch the progress of the nesting cycle, as the tiny, helpless, just-hatched babies become adorable fluffy older nestlings.

Make sure to keep careful records so you know how old the young are. Keep a record book or a set of record cards (see next page). It helps to number your boxes. We write the number in permanent marker on the front of the box, under the eave, so it is not exposed to the weather.

Familiarize yourself with the normal sequence of events in the bluebird breeding cycle by reading the chapters on bluebird behavior later in this book. In this way you will more quickly recognize any problems signaled by changes in the birds' behavior.

If all goes well, the young should fledge at 16–23 days, depending on the species and a variety of other conditions mentioned in the chapter on nestlings. After the young fledge, the nest will be flattened out and fairly clean, with maybe just a few droppings. (In mountain bluebird nests, there

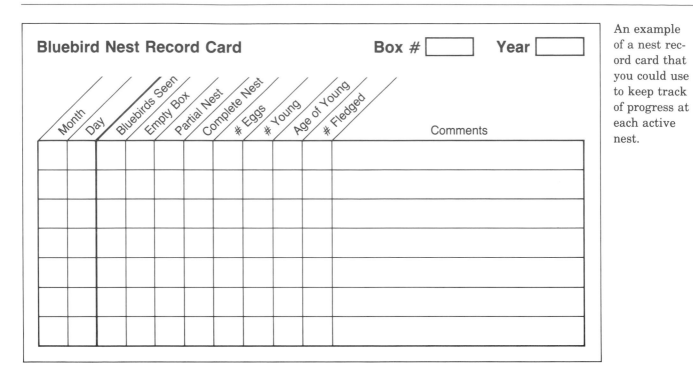

Bluebird Nest Record Card   Box # [   ]   Year [   ]

An example of a nest record card that you could use to keep track of progress at each active nest.

Month	Day	Bluebirds Seen	Empty Box	Partial Nest	Complete Nest	# Eggs	# Young	Age of Young	# Fledged	Comments

may be quite a few droppings left.) If there has been predation, the nest is often torn up (see Protection from Predators, page 50).

Handling Problems

Occasionally when monitoring, you encounter problems. Even though it can be upsetting when something goes wrong, you should be aware of potential problems so that you will be able to take steps to solve them.

If there are signs of predation, such as the disappearance of eggs, young, or the incubating adult, or the destruction of the nest, learn how to interpret who has done it and take steps to predator-proof (see pages 50–53). If you ever find a dead young in the nest but the others are still alive, remove the dead bird from the box.

Bluebirds are curious about and will inspect any hole that looks like the entrance to a cavity, including potentially lethal places like stovepipes. Cap stovepipes, chimney flues, and so forth with a piece of ½-inch hardware cloth.

Abandoned Young or Eggs

It is sometimes hard to tell if eggs have been abandoned, and there is not much you can do about it if they are. During egg laying, which usually takes place over a period of several days, the female does not stay near the nest during the day, so the eggs will be cool and unattended.

Once the female begins incubation, she remains fairly constantly at the box, taking short breaks to get food for herself. If you monitor while she is on a break from incubating, the eggs will usually be warm to the touch. Even if they are cool to the touch it does not mean the female has abandoned them. There are times, particularly in cool weather when the female may stay off the nest for a while, that the eggs will cool. If she does not remain off too long, they still will hatch. In cases like this, the incubation period may be longer.

Only the female can incubate the eggs. If she dies, the male cannot take over, so the eggs will die. However, once the young have hatched, if one parent dies the other is perfectly capable of raising the young alone. The young can only be considered to be abandoned if both parents are known to have died or abandoned the nest.

The only sure way to know that young are abandoned is to watch the nest for at least 4 hours to make sure that the parents have not visited it. Abandoned young will be weak and may be cold, but they can survive about 24 hours without food.

If you are sure they have been abandoned, call

the local or national bluebird society, the Audubon Society, or a bird rehabilitation center. You cannot raise the young birds yourself; it is against the law. They can be raised legally only by someone who is licensed with a special permit from the U.S. Fish and Wildlife Service, or the Canadian counterpart.

Caring for Young in an Emergency

If you have to care for young bluebirds in an emergency situation, while you are getting them to a licensed rehabilitator, here are some tips. First of all, keep them warm. Warm them in your hands or by putting them next to your body until you get them home; then keep them in a warm place in a small box with a nest made out of soft tissues. They should be fed every 20 minutes, dawn to dusk. They can be fed mealworms (available in pet stores), earthworm pieces, canned dog food, canned puppy food, small pieces of ground beef, or scrambled or hard-boiled egg yolk. Offer food on blunt tweezers, giving small young tiny bits of food and more developed young larger pieces. Do not try to force-feed young when they are cold; warm them up first.

Lillian carefully monitoring a bluebird nest box on one of our trails.

Bad Weather

Cold, rainy weather can be responsible for the death of young and adults. If it is too cold to get food, the young can starve and so can adults. This is especially true during the nestling stage of 5–9 days old, when the female has stopped brooding the nestlings but they are still susceptible to cold. If they cool to the point that they do not lift their heads to receive food from the parents, then the parents may abandon them. Sometimes, just to save themselves, the adults must leave the area and try to find food. Often, though, if the adults survive, they will return and successfully renest, for their nesting instinct is strong. There have even been cases in which they renested on top of old nests.

In bad weather it may be possible to help the bluebirds by putting out supplemental food. Try putting mealworms or raisins in a small cup or coffee-can lid nailed to a stake near the nest box. (See the chapter Bluebird Feeders, page 36.)

After Fledging

After you are sure that the nestlings have left the nest, take out the old nest right away. Put the old nest and any debris from the box into a trash bag and remove it from the area. Old nests left on the ground below the bird box could attract predators. The female may build a new nest within a week. If she has already started building a new nest on top of the old, then leave it there. The female will go about starting another brood while the male still feeds the fledglings from the previous brood.

After the last brood of the season has fledged, clean out all houses. Check them in winter to make sure no mice are in them, for mouse urine and droppings can foul the boxes. Some bluebirders choose to plug box holes in the winter to keep out mice. But this also keeps bluebirds from using the boxes as roosting spots on cold nights. In areas where bluebirds overwinter, leave the entrance holes unplugged.

DEALING WITH COMPETITORS

Bluebirds First

The goal of setting up a bluebird trail is to make it as attractive as possible — but only to bluebirds. In addition to having good boxes in good habitat, you must also discourage the competition. We wish it were as easy as putting up a little sign that said "Only bluebirds permitted," but that is not the case. You need to understand who the potential competitors are, and what can be done, when possible, to limit the competition.

House sparrows are one of the most common competitors with bluebirds for nest boxes. Female on left, male on right.

House Sparrows

House sparrows are the biggest competitor, and in some cases predator, of bluebirds. These ubiquitous birds, sometimes called English Sparrows, are not native, but were introduced to the United States in 1850. They have expanded their range across the continent, and they are aggressive and successful competitors for nesting cavities with our native birds.

Male sparrows have strong attachments to their nest sites. They claim a nest site by stuffing it with nesting material such as weeds, grasses, string, feathers, and bits of paper and cloth. This may start as early as late fall, but usually occurs in late winter or early spring. At the nest site the male repeatedly sings "chirup chireep, chirup" to attract a female. Both birds build the final nest, with the female laying 4–6 eggs, which are whitish, gray, or greenish with brown irregular spots. They are incubated for 12 days, primarily by the female; once hatched, the nestlings remain in the nest for 15–17 days.

Many people think sparrows are cute and cannot understand why anyone would not want them in nest boxes. Sparrows may be cute, but they are also usually much more aggressive than bluebirds. They will attack and kill bluebird adults and young and also destroy their eggs to get at a nest box.

House sparrows have adapted to many other places besides nest boxes in which they can nest, such as any nook or cranny in buildings in urban or rural areas. It is important that they not be allowed to use bluebird nest boxes, for bluebirds, in contrast, have very few other places in which they can nest.

The following are ways that you can keep house sparrows from using bluebird nest boxes.

1. Don't put up bluebird boxes in a known

house sparrow habitat, such as urban areas, or horse or cattle farms where sparrows are known to be living.

2. Constantly remove house sparrow nests and eggs from your nest boxes. This should be done at least every week, and it may take many weeks to discourage them. This has been an effective method for us on our trails.

Note: Because house sparrows are not a native species they (and also starlings) are not protected by law, as are all of our native birds. Therefore, it is legal to remove their nests and eggs. Make sure you have correctly identified house sparrows and their nests before taking action. See the nest identification illustration in this chapter.

3. Many bluebirders recommend trapping and removing house sparrows if they continue to be a problem. You need to trap the male, since he will remain faithful to the nest site even if the female disappears, but the female will desert the nest if the male is removed.

At least once an hour, check your trap so that you do not inadvertently catch or hurt any native species of bird, since they are protected by law. When relocating a sparrow, take it more than 5 miles away and preferably to an urban area, or someplace that is not a favorable bluebird habitat.

There are traps, such as the Huber Sparrow Trap, that fit in an individual nest box. There are also big traps that will catch many sparrows while they feed on the ground. See Resources, page 96, for where to buy traps.

Starlings

Starlings are also an imported species. They were introduced into North America in 1890 and immediately became aggressive competitors with bluebirds for nest cavities. The good news is that starlings are larger than bluebirds and cannot fit through the 1½-inch or 1⁹⁄₁₆-inch entrance hole of a bluebird box. Any nest box entrance larger than this will let starlings move right in.

Rarely, a starling clings to the entrance of a bluebird nest box and pokes its beak partway into the hole and may attempt to harm the young. This is more of a problem when bluebirds build their nest so high that the young are close to the

Tree swallows are beautiful birds that often compete with bluebirds for nest sites. However, there are ways to provide for both of these lovely birds in your area.

entrance hole. In this case, bluebirders recommend that the nest be lowered by gently removing some of the grass underneath the nest.

Swallows

Two species of swallows compete with bluebirds for nest boxes: tree swallows, which live throughout North America, and violet-green swallows, which live only in the West. These are beautiful and beneficial native birds that eat many insects. Tree swallows are iridescent blue-black on top with white underparts. Violet-green swallows are iridescent green on top with white underparts and white on their cheek and above the eye. Both swallows build nests of grasses lined with feathers. The nest of the violet-green swallow may also contain straw, string, and hair. The eggs of both species are pure white.

Swallows are fairly even competitors with bluebirds. Swallows sometimes usurp bluebird nests and occasionally bluebirds take over swallow nests. These takeovers can result in the loss of eggs, nestlings, and (rarely) even adults. When

Nest identification. Knowing these five common nests will help you record what has happened in your birdhouses. These houses were opened up after the breeding season for this picture. Here are some clues to recognizing each species' nest. Chickadee or titmouse: moss, fur, and other downy materials. House sparrow: feathers mixed into a jumble of grasses, cloth, and other odds and ends. Bluebird: a nicely made nest of mostly grasses or pine needles. Tree swallow: a nest of grasses that is just lined with feathers. House wren: a nest of solid twigs, sometimes lined with finer fibers.

several pairs of swallows are in the same area, they may gang up on the bluebirds, and in these cases bluebirds generally lose. In some areas of the country, bluebirds arrive at nest boxes well ahead of swallows in the spring, and this gives them a competitive advantage.

The best way to alleviate some of this competition is to put up nest boxes in pairs, placing the boxes about 5–15 feet apart. The swallows are territorial and will defend both boxes from other swallows, but they will defend only the box they are actually nesting in from other species. This leaves the other box available for other species of birds, such as bluebirds. Pairing boxes has worked on our bluebird trail; where once we had only tree swallows, they and bluebirds now nest 5 feet apart.

Additionally, keep each pair of boxes about 50–100 yards from any other pair of boxes. This cuts down on the density of swallows in the area, which enables the bluebirds to defend a box more easily.

The problem is more complicated in the West, where both species of swallows are competing with bluebirds. Some people have tried placing boxes in groups of three in these areas, but this method gets mixed reviews.

There are reports of swallows nesting closer than 5 feet apart and, in some cases, in boxes that were paired back to back.

Wrens

House wrens, found across most of North America, are small brown birds that are a competitor and, occasionally, a predator of bluebirds (see page 51). The male house wren claims one or several boxes and makes "dummy" nests, stuffing them with twigs. When a female arrives, she chooses one as the nest site and adds the final lining.

Carolina and Bewick's wrens also may compete with bluebirds for nest boxes, although not as often, since these two species can nest in other locations, such as in shrubs, nooks, and crevices. Bewick's wrens, like house wrens, make several dummy nests. The eggs of all three wrens are whitish heavily speckled with brown.

The best way to reduce competition between bluebirds and house wrens is to place bluebird nest boxes well away from good wren habitat. House wrens prefer woody, brushy areas, so place bluebird nest boxes at least 100 feet from such habitats.

Wasps and Ants

Paper wasps and yellow jackets, of the genus *Polistes,* start building their gray, papery nests on the ceilings of nest boxes in early spring. Before this, these wasps may roost together in the box each night. Birds are reluctant to use a box that is occupied by wasps.

Check under the roof of your nest boxes for wasps. We find the easiest way to deal with wasps is to monitor the boxes in early spring mornings when the temperature is 50°F or lower and the wasps are too cool to fly or move quickly.

They can be crushed and their nests cleaned out with a putty knife or a blunt stick. This may have to be repeated several times. Some people rub petroleum jelly or a bar of Ivory soap or liquid hand soap on the ceilings of boxes to deter the wasps from attaching their nests. Another method is to spray the wasps through the entrance hole at night with pyrethrin spray (no greater than 0.1 percent concentration) and then plug the hole, being sure to unplug it and remove the wasps in the morning. Pyrethrin spray in this low concentration is nontoxic to bluebirds. It is available in pet stores as a spray for caged birds. Do not use any chemical other than pyrethrin.

Ants too sometimes inhabit bluebird boxes. See the chapter on predators, page 52, for control of ants and fire ants.

Other Competitors

Many other species of birds use nest boxes, but only a few can get into an entrance hole 1 9/16 inches or 1½ inches in diameter. Some of the more common species include chickadees, titmice, nuthatches, house finches, and some flycatchers.

Pairing boxes 5–15 feet apart is a good way to accommodate both swallows and bluebirds.

Most of these species nest in wooded areas and are smaller than bluebirds. In general, they cannot defend boxes against bluebirds.

In the West, however, the ash-throated flycatcher occasionally usurps bluebird nests. Sometimes they break the eggs, but other times they just lay their brown, speckled eggs right on top of the bluebird eggs. There is even a case in which an ash-throated flycatcher laid her own 5 eggs over 2 existing bluebird eggs and hatched and raised all 7 nestlings. Brown-headed cowbirds have also been known to lay their eggs in bluebird nests (see page 75).

White-footed mice and deer mice may build their nests of fine shredded material in nest boxes and live there. Clean out all mouse nests (don't be surprised if the mouse jumps out) in early spring before bluebirds arrive, or plug up the nest box holes in winter to keep them out.

Flying squirrels may move into nest boxes and can eat bluebird eggs. Since flying squirrels only live in wooded habitats, keep bluebird boxes at least 100 feet away from tall trees.

PROTECTION FROM PREDATORS

Predation

When monitoring your bluebird trail you may come across evidence of predation. This can be difficult emotionally, but it is something all bluebirders must face. Rarely does a bluebird trail have a 100 percent success rate.

Predation is part of nature, and we must learn to accept it. There are, however, many things you can do to lessen predation on your bluebird trail. Here is a list of the kind of predators you may encounter, the signs of predation associated with each, and how you can control them. Detailed descriptions of the various predator guards follow.

House Sparrows — House sparrows can be vicious predators of bluebirds. They can enter a nest box and kill adults or young by pecking open their skulls or pecking out their eyes, and they can destroy eggs by pecking or removing them. The best way to control them is to remove their nests and eggs repeatedly and, if necessary, trap and relocate them. See Dealing with Competitors, pages 46–47.

Cats — Cats can climb posts, reach into nest boxes, and harm the young, or they can sit on the top of the box and harass or kill the adults. They can also sit on the ground in front of the box and jump up to catch the adults, but they can be de-

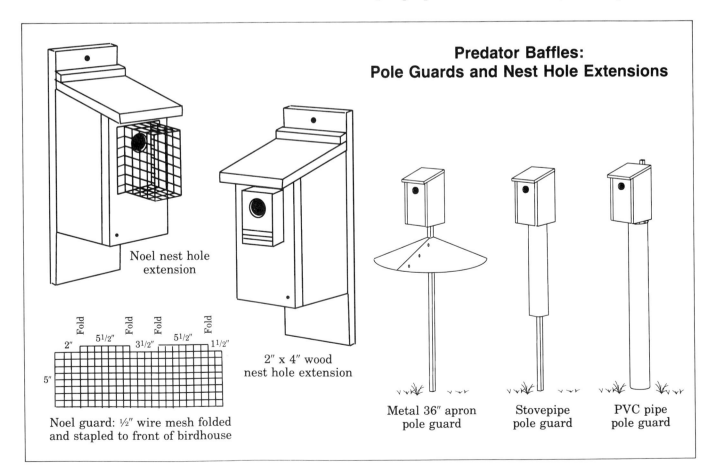

**Predator Baffles:
Pole Guards and Nest Hole Extensions**

Noel nest hole extension

2" x 4" wood nest hole extension

Noel guard: ½" wire mesh folded and stapled to front of birdhouse

Fold   Fold   Fold   Fold

2"   5½"   3½"   5½"   1½"

5"

Metal 36" apron pole guard

Stovepipe pole guard

PVC pipe pole guard

Raccoons are often more common in suburban than rural areas. Nest boxes must be protected from them with predator guards on the pole or nest box entrance.

terred from this by your mounting the boxes 8 feet high on poles. When possible, cats should be confined during nesting season and should be prevented from climbing nest box poles through the use of predator guards.

Raccoons — Raccoons are major predators of bluebirds. They climb to boxes at night and kill any adults, young, or eggs that are in the box. A nest that has been disturbed by a raccoon will be missing birds or eggs and the nesting material will be pulled partway through the entrance hole. Frequently, claw marks are found on the box, and feathers and bits of eggs are scattered on the ground below. Occasionally, raccoons leave few signs of their predation. Deter raccoons with predator guards on the poles or entrance hole extensions. Boxes mounted on trees or fence posts are not as easily protected from raccoons.

Snakes — Snakes, especially those of the genus *Elaphe,* such as rat snakes, and those of the genus *Pituophis,* such as bull snakes and pine-gopher snakes, are predators of bluebirds in many parts of the country. One study showed that snake predation occurred more within 300 feet of woods. Snakes climb up poles, even poles that are greased or spread with Tanglefoot (a sticky substance available at garden supply stores), and eat young and eggs. There is often no sign of distur-

bance to the nest. Snakes can be deterred by 4-inch PVC pipe or specific snake traps.

Wrens — Wrens, especially house wrens, can prey on bluebirds by puncturing and/or removing eggs. The eggs may have tiny puncture holes and sometimes are thrown on the ground or taken elsewhere. In some cases wrens have killed adults or killed nestlings and thrown them on the ground. The best protection from wrens is to keep the bluebird trail away from wren habitat (see pages 48–49).

Hawks — Hawks can kill adult and fledgling bluebirds as they fly about the nest box. Kestrels have been reported to cling to an entrance hole of 1¾ inches, reach in, and remove a 6-day-old nestling. Sharp-shinned hawks, Cooper's hawks, and merlins eat mainly birds and can eat bluebirds. Sharp-shinned hawks have been reported to catch adult bluebirds as they left the nest box. For protection from hawks, place boxes away from known nesting hawks and away from power lines and other perches above the box from which hawks can dive down and surprise the adults.

Other Mammals — White-footed mice and deer mice often nest in bluebird boxes, and they might eat the eggs or young. We had a bluebird pair desert a box with eggs after a mouse moved in. The mouse did not eat the eggs, but it lived in the box and left little piles of chewed seeds. Chipmunks, opossums, and weasels are also capable of climbing to nests and eating eggs or young.

Red, Douglas, and gray squirrels sometimes enlarge nest holes through gnawing, in an attempt to use the nest box for their own nest. Most nest boxes are too small, and after getting in they abandon them. They can also destroy eggs and young. If the entrance holes are reinforced with a metal plate or nest hole extension, the squirrels cannot chew through.

The best way to stop all of these climbing predators is to use predator guards on the poles.

Other Birds — Crows, blue jays, and grackles prey on eggs and nestlings of birds that build open cup nests, but they rarely prey on birds in nest boxes with 1½-inch entrance holes. However, in certain areas of the West, magpies have become problems at bluebird boxes.

Blowflies — Blowflies are a type of fly that lay their eggs in bird nests. The eggs hatch and the young flies, called larvae or maggots, suck the blood of the nestling bluebirds. They do this at night; during the day they crawl down and hide in the nesting material. Blowfly maggots are oval and grayish and grow to about ⅜ inch long. They then turn into pupae, which look like black capsules about ⅜ inch long. In 10–14 days they emerge as adult flies. Blowflies do not usually kill bluebirds unless there is a large infestation.

To check for blowflies, lift up the bottom of the nest, gently tap it, and carefully look through the nest material. If you find any blowfly larvae or pupae, brush them out. In cases where there are a large number of larvae, 50–100 or more, fashion a new nest out of clean, dry grass, remove the old nest, and put the babies in the new nest.

Some bluebirders have tried putting little platforms of ⅜-inch hardware cloth 1 inch up from the bottom of the box. The bluebird builds a nest on top of it; theoretically, the larvae fall through the hardware cloth and are not able to climb back into the nest. Others have found this to be ineffective, for many larvae always remain in the nest material where it is densest, just below the cup.

Ants — Ants may occasionally nest in the bluebird box and in some cases can even eat the young. Once ants are breeding in the nest, you

Blowfly larvae, which are grayish, and the pupae, which are black. These should be removed from nests during the nestling phase.

must remove the nest and ants, build a new nest, and replace the birds. Also use Tanglefoot or grease on the mounting pole to prevent ants from climbing it.

In the South, there are fire ants that prey on nestlings. They can be stopped from reaching the box by making a barrier between the box and mounting pole. Put the long mounting nails or screws at the top and bottom of the box's back through wooden thread spools and coat the spools with STP Oil Treatment; it does not harden even in hot weather, unlike other grease, and prevents the ants from crossing. Some people use automobile chassis grease mixed with a little turpentine to coat the barrier, or smear it on the mounting pole.

Other Insects — Sometimes blackflies and gnats can be present in large numbers and bite the young. They may be annoying but do not cause death. Mites, fleas, and lice have been found in bluebird boxes but rarely are any problem. If their numbers build up too much, spray the box with low-concentration (0.1 percent) pyrethrin spray after the bluebirds have fledged from the box.

Predator Guards

There are two main types of predator guards: those that prevent the predator from climbing up the mounting pole, and those that prevent the predator from reaching into the box.

Pole Guards — A guard around or attached to the nest box pole can prevent climbing predators such as raccoons, cats, snakes, and mammals from reaching the box in the first place. One of the most effective is a length of 4-inch-diameter PVC pipe placed over the entire length of the mounting pole from just under the nest box to the ground. This should be greased with automobile or marine grease or Vaseline. The grease may have to be reapplied several times if it hardens.

Some people attach a 2-foot length of 4-inch PVC pipe or metal stovepipe directly to the bottom of the nest box below the birdhouse. If a predator climbs up the pole, it cannot get by this section because it cannot get a grip.

Another device is a 36-inch metal cone that attaches to the pole, open end down, directly below the nest box. This is very effective. Some people have found that mounting their poles on greased metal pipe is effective for most climbing predators except snakes.

For snakes, you can sheathe the pole with ungreased 4-inch-diameter PVC pipe, then put several shovelfuls of sand around the base. There is also a type of live snake trap, the Krueger snake trap, that is made out of mesh that can be placed around the pole (see Resources, page 96).

Boxes mounted on trees, wooden posts, or telephone poles are harder to predator-proof. You must wrap the post (or pole or trunk) with a 3-foot-wide strip of galvanized metal. Keep it smooth so there are no gripping places. Make sure any tree on which a box is mounted does not connect with other trees at the canopy, because a raccoon could reach the box via another tree.

Nest Hole Extensions — There are some devices that attach directly to the nest box, extending out from the entrance hole, and make it difficult for a predator to reach down into the nest. One is a rectangular frame of fine mesh hardware cloth, called the Noel guard, for which plans are given in this chapter. Another is a plastic 3-inch-long tube with a 1½-inch diameter that snaps onto the hole.

A male eastern bluebird that is thriving and raising young.

In tests, the Noel guard seemed readily accepted by birds before nesting and when it was put on after they had started nesting. In contrast, we have had bluebirds reject the plastic tube guard during nest-building and egg-laying phases and refuse to enter the nest, although there are other reports of bluebirds successfully using it.

Some bluebirders have had good success using a 2-inch-thick block of wood with a hole in the middle the same size as the entrance hole; this is placed on the box over the entrance hole before the birds nest. Other people have experimented with very deep boxes to make it difficult for predators to reach the young. These nest hole extensions may not be accepted by all birds, but when it is not possible to protect the box any other way — for instance, when it is mounted on a fence post — they are certainly worth a try.

BLUEBIRD FLIGHT

Flights of Fancy

It is fun to watch bluebirds fly, for their flight varies depending on what the birds are doing. In short trips to and from their nest box and from perch to perch, they move their wings very rapidly, giving their flight a fluttery, mothlike appearance. But when bluebirds take off high in the air for longer distances, their flight is strong and continuous and their wings move at a slower beat.

The aerial agility of bluebirds also enables them to use flight for many different purposes in their lives. For example, they use flight in three ways while feeding.

All three species can "hawk" insects by flying out from a perch to catch them in midair. This is similar to the way flycatchers get insects. All three species also have the ability to hover as they search for food on the ground. This ability is particularly well developed in the mountain bluebird, which actually has longer wings in relation to body size than the other two species, possibly as an adaptation to feeding in more open areas where there are fewer natural perches. Some observers liken the mountain bluebird's hovering to that of the American kestrel, a small falcon that hovers over fields to look for prey.

Normal feeding of bluebirds is accomplished by short flights from a perch to the ground and back,

A female eastern bluebird landing at a perch after a short flight to the ground for food.

A female eastern bluebird just grabbing hold of the rim of the nest entrance while landing with food for her young.

A male eastern bluebird breaking the speed of his flight while preparing to land at the nest.

all within a matter of seconds. In fact, this kind of "drop feeding" is so characteristic of bluebirds that it can be a good way to identify the birds from a distance.

Bluebirds need a great deal of skill to land directly at the entrance of a cavity or nest box. In the pictures in this chapter you can see some of the extraordinary maneuverings they do as they accomplish this feat.

Bluebirds also use flight as part of their communication system. A particularly rapid wing action is used in a special flight that is part of courtship. And one or both wings may be lifted while the bird is perched, in the wing-wave display. In addition, sometimes one member of a pair will deviate from its route to the nest box and fly close over its perched mate as if to call attention to its presence. In response, the perched bird may do wing-wave. (See Bluebird Language, page 56.)

Fighting can also occur during flight. Occasionally, during breeding, rival bluebirds may fly at one another in an attack. Or, if the rivals are vying for one mate, nest box, or territory, they may face each other and fight while hovering in midair.

A female eastern bluebird getting ready to grasp a foothold at the nest entrance.

BLUEBIRD LANGUAGE

Bird Language

Birds communicate with one another through the use of sounds and gestures. This communication enables them to coordinate their lives so that they can successfully breed and survive. Bird language is, of course, not as detailed as our own, by any means, and does not express thoughts and ideas. Rather, it is an expression of certain emotional states or a signal of simple relationships and intents. The various sounds and communicative gestures that birds make are called auditory and visual displays. Birds have to be studied closely in order for us to recognize and understand their displays. The language of bluebirds is only partially understood, and all three species need to be studied more in this regard, especially mountain and western bluebirds.

A male eastern bluebird doing the wing-wave display.

Auditory Displays

Bluebirds are generally quiet birds and do not rely heavily on sound for communication. The context and possible meanings of their most common sounds are listed below.

Song — Song is given by both sexes, but most often by the male, who uses it to announce his presence on the territory to neighboring males, to initially attract a female, and to get his mate's attention.

When given toward other males, it is aggressive in intent. Often, neighboring males sing back and forth, alternating songs. Once neighbors have agreed on territorial boundaries, song is less often used in this way.

When a male does not have a mate during the breeding season, either because he has not yet attracted one or because his mate has died, then he will start singing from the tops of trees. At this time song can be very loud and carry hundreds of yards. Once he attracts a female, he becomes much quieter and does not sing from high perches.

When a territory and mate are acquired, song by the male or female is soft and only heard from 20 to 40 yards away. It then seems to be used as a communication between the pair and sometimes is given during mild disturbances, such as when a person approaches the nest or fledglings. In these instances the female may sing, and this may in turn attract the male for defense of the nest or young.

In most birds, song is a longer, more musical, and more complex sound than the same species' calls. In bluebirds, this is not as clear-cut. Song is often just several calls strung together in a longer sequence.

The eastern bluebird's song sounds like the words "cheer cheerful charmer" or "ch'ch'cheer cheerful charmer." It is a series of 6–8 short, low-pitched, melodious whistles.

The song of the western bluebird is higher pitched than that of the mountain or eastern bluebird and contains three main sounds — "cheer," a rapid "churchur," and a short "chup." Various combinations of these sounds are given in short sequences during song.

The mountain bluebird's song consists of a rapid "churchur," a slow "chur-chur," a short "chup," and a rattling "churrrrr." As in the western bluebird, these are strung together into short sequences. A loud and more forceful version that sounds more like the song of a robin may be given just before dawn.

Calls — Calls of bluebirds fall into two categories: those that seem to be the syllables of the song used singly, and harsher, short chips. The syllables of the song, such as "churchur" or "cheer," often seem to function as contact notes between the pair or among members of a feeding flock, enabling the birds to keep in touch and co-ordinate their activities. In the eastern bluebird this call sounds like "turawee"; in the western bluebird it can sound like "chweer"; and in the mountain bluebird it sounds like "chur-chur."

The short, harsh call may be given singly or in a series, making a rapid chattering. This call is usually given in moments of alarm, such as when another bluebird intrudes on a territory or there is danger nearby. Both calls are given by male and female. Audible bill-snapping can also occur during situations of alarm or aggression.

Visual Displays

Visual displays are often used by bluebirds. The two main ones are listed below. They are done by all three species. Other actions that could also be considered visual displays are described in the chapters on territory (page 60) and courtship (page 64).

Wing-wave — This is the most common visual display of bluebirds. In it the bird lifts one or both wings in a quick wave while perched. Wings may also be quivered momentarily. It is done by male and female during breeding and seems to function as a kind of greeting or attention-getter. The male does it at the nest entrance and on top of

A male mountain bluebird with food for the young. During breeding season, the parents use contact calls to coordinate their activities.

the box and sometimes when he has food for the female. Both birds do wing-wave as the other flies overhead or near. And wing-wave is often given when the two land near each other on a perch or at the nest box.

Flight Display — Bluebirds can deviate from their normal flight pattern as a method of communication. This is done mostly by the male during territory formation and courtship. In one type of flight display he uses slow, deep wingbeats; in another he flies with a lopsided flight; in a third he hovers in front of the nest hole. All of these displays seem to call attention to his presence or to the nest box, and this may be their main function. Sometimes these flights are accompanied by song.

SPRING ARRIVAL

When Do They Return?

When bluebirds return to your nest boxes depends on the species, your geographic location, the weather, and the experience level of your bluebirds. In other words, there is no easy answer at any given spot.

Each species differs in its timetable. Where their ranges overlap, mountain bluebirds may arrive up to 2 weeks ahead of eastern bluebirds. In areas where both western and mountain bluebirds live, they may arrive together in mixed flocks, but the mountain bluebird starts nesting earlier. The mountain bluebird is the best of the three species in adapting to cold weather and may start breeding even during late winter blizzards.

Geographic location is equally important. In the southern portion of the eastern bluebird's range, the birds often winter near where they breed and may occasionally show up at the breeding ground in winter. Eastern bluebirds that breed farther north may have to migrate there in spring and thus often do not show up until just before breeding.

Weather affects the availability of berries and insects on which bluebirds feed, and this in turn affects their movement back to breeding grounds. Cold and rainy weather can delay their migration north. For example, mountain and western bluebirds arrive on breeding grounds in the North anytime from early February to late March depending on the severity of the weather; in warmer weather they appear earlier.

Experience is also an interesting influence on bluebirds' spring arrival. In our own area of Massachusetts, some eastern bluebirds that have bred there before remain nearby in winter and return to nesting areas as early as February. But just a few miles away, there are areas where bluebirds have not nested for 20 years. One re-

A male eastern bluebird perched among the emerging spring leaves of a tulip tree.

cent spring, bluebirds showed up at these spots to nest but not until the first week in May. These later birds were using the area for the first time, were not as experienced, and were just building a nest at the same time other, experienced bluebirds in the nearby towns were already feeding nestlings.

In general, you can look for bluebirds to arrive on breeding areas starting in mid-February at the earliest and on into June at the latest.

Returning Birds

Bluebirds may return to breeding grounds as lone birds, as pairs, and as small flocks. Lone birds may scout out an area and then leave and come back with a mate. Pairs will stay if they find a suitable nest site. And flocks wander about more generally, with no aggressive interactions; then, after about a week in the area, they seem to break up into separate breeding pairs.

There have been various estimates of the percentage of bluebirds that return to previous nesting sites. In general, bluebirds return to successful nesting areas. A study of mountain bluebirds found 54 percent of the females to return to the same territory and the same box. This is high considering there is undoubtedly some mortality to be factored in. Other studies have shown about a 30 percent return. If a pair are unsuccessful at one nest site, they generally move to another.

Young bluebirds in their first breeding year often nest near where they were raised. It is believed that they may return to the general area of their birth and then explore outward from there for their own nest site. They may even prefer to breed at a site similar to the one in which they were raised, even to the point of picking a similar-style nest box.

A male western bluebird with a bit of food at a potential nest site.

Start of Breeding Activities

Just because bluebirds arrive at their breeding grounds does not mean they will start breeding immediately. Again, there is tremendous variety and individuality in their behavior. Bluebirds are notorious for showing up and then leaving, then showing up, and then leaving again. It can drive a bluebirder crazy.

Much of this coming and going in the early stages may have to do with food. On warm days the birds may try to feed near their nest site. When the weather is cold or rainy for a spell, they may have to give up on insects and feed on berries, which may mean leaving to go to a berry-rich location.

Even after doing some nest building early in the season, they may abandon the area for another spot. The name of the game is variability.

Just about any combination of events may occur, and the more you watch the birds and record their activities, the more new examples you will find.

If it is spring and you are wondering if bluebirds will ever show up at your boxes, remember that bluebirds can have up to three broods in one breeding season and that eggs have been found in nests as late as early August. Thus, you have many months in which you can still hope for nesting bluebirds. Don't give up!

TERRITORY

Bluebird Territories

During the breeding season, bluebirds defend territories on which they tend to remain and carry out all of their activities, including nesting, mating, and feeding. Bluebird territories vary in size depending on the availability of food and nest holes and on the amount of pressure from other bluebirds trying to nest in the same area. With sufficient food and a good nest hole, a bluebird territory can be as small as 2 acres.

However, a bluebird pair will not limit themselves to this small an area unless there is pressure from neighboring pairs of bluebirds. Lacking this pressure, a pair may wander as much as a quarter mile from their nest site. In one telemetry study, three eastern bluebird territories were measured at 2.1, 2.7, and 3.5 acres, the smallest being a territory bordered on all but one side by other bluebird territories.

As a rule, bluebirds do not nest closer than 100 yards from each other, but there are many exceptions to this. Eastern bluebirds have been found nesting as close as 200 feet. One record for density of nesting bluebirds occurred in Colorado. In an area of just about 1.75 acres were found 6 mountain bluebird nests and 2 western bluebird nests. In the same small grove of aspens were 6 tree swallow nests, 1 violet-green swallow nest, and 1 house wren nest.

Territories are defended against other bluebirds from the time of arrival of a lone male or pair in spring through the fledging of the last brood in late summer. In some cases adult or even juvenile males may briefly defend boxes in fall.

Territorial Behavior

The initial outlining of a territory is a gradual process. Individual males or mated pairs arrive on the breeding ground, usually near areas where they bred previously, and start to explore nest boxes and natural cavities. As they become more attached to the area, each male begins to do two things: sing frequently from exposed perches and fly from perch to perch around the limits of his territory. Both of these behaviors seem to help make his presence known to neighboring males.

When territories are adjacent, the two resident males may perch near the common border and alternate singing; this is sometimes referred to as song duels.

A male mountain bluebird peering from a possible nest site in his territory.

A male eastern bluebird pausing as he circulates about his territory.

A female mountain bluebird. She will defend the area near the nest from other females.

Both male and female defend the territory, with the female confining most of her defense to the nest site and its immediate surroundings. During interactions, male bluebirds chase other males off their territory but do not chase off females; and in turn, females chase other females but not males.

Scientists have come up with an interesting explanation for this behavior. It may be that a male does not want other males to mate with his female and at the same time wants to optimize his chances of mating with a strange female. The same is true of a female; she does not want other females mating with her mate and possibly dumping eggs in her nest, but she also wants to leave open her chances of mating with another male that might come into her territory. For more on this, see page 66 and page 75.

At first, intruders are often other pairs looking for nest boxes. Pairs may compete over a nest box

for up to 2 weeks. Later in the nesting season, intruders are usually lone males flying high over the territory and dropping down near the nest site.

Territory holders react to intruding bluebirds in several ways. One is to fly to the nest box and either enter it or perch on it. Or the resident bird may position itself between the box and the intruder. In either of these cases, the resident may sing, possibly to intimidate the intruder.

In other cases, the resident bird will fly toward the intruder, giving alarm notes. This may make the intruder leave. If not, then the resident bird may chase the intruder for up to 15 minutes. In these interactions too, the resident pair usually position themselves between the intruder and their nest box.

Once birds are settled on territories, there is little other interaction with other bluebirds, except for neighboring males' sometimes meeting briefly at common borders.

Where Species' Ranges Overlap

There are certain regions of North America where more than one species of bluebird breeds in the same location. In areas of Washington and Montana, western bluebirds and mountain bluebirds nest side by side. Both species tend to arrive on the breeding ground at the same time, but the western bluebirds become attached to specific nest sites earlier and immediately begin to defend the territory. The mountain bluebirds explore for a week or two more before settling down.

In these areas, each species defends its territory against its own and the other species. This is called interspecific territoriality, and it is rare among our common birds. Neither the western nor the mountain bluebird is clearly dominant over the other.

In regions where mountain and eastern bluebirds both breed, interspecific territoriality again occurs. The mountain bluebird tends to arrive several weeks ahead of the eastern bluebird. It also seems to be the case that mountain bluebirds have a slight edge over eastern bluebirds during territorial interactions.

This slight dominance is sometimes used to explain changes in the relative populations where

A male western bluebird on a brief trip to the ground for food.

two bluebird species overlap, but it is not as simple as this. Population changes can be caused by a variety of other factors, such as the number of available nest boxes, the habitat, weather patterns, food abundance, and the populations of predators and competitors.

Individual Species Behavior

Among mountain bluebirds, if an intruding bluebird does not respond to the direct flight and alarm calls of the resident, then the resident may engage in hover-flight, in which it hovers over the intruder and audibly snaps its beak. Or both bluebirds may fly slowly toward each other, hovering as they meet face to face, and slowly rising several feet into the air. If the intruder still refuses to leave, then the two may even lock feet and tumble to the ground pecking at each other. This extreme defensive behavior occurs only rarely.

The eastern bluebird's territorial defense may include still other behaviors. The male may make semicircular flights up over the territory; he may do a slow, stalling flight or a straight, rapid flight accompanied by song while flying from perch to perch or nest box to nest box; and he may perch at a nest box entrance with tail spread and poke his head repeatedly into the entrance hole.

In one case, a western bluebird male was extremely aggressive toward humans and avian intruders. When his box was monitored, he would hover over the people, snap his beak, and dive down at them. This behavior is fairly common in mountain bluebirds but unusual for eastern bluebirds, which usually just fly a few yards away and wait quietly when their nest boxes are monitored.

In another instance, immature male western bluebirds defended nest boxes by perching on top of them and flying out at other birds that came near. This occurred just after the breeding season, in late summer and early fall. They seemed to defend the boxes from other male bluebirds, not so much their parents or siblings as other immature and adult bluebirds wandering through. The behavior lasted only a few weeks.

COURTSHIP

The Start of Pairing

When bluebirds first arrive on their territory, it may be as either lone males or as pairs from the previous season. In many cases, males arrive a week or two before the females and start to defend territories in favorable habitats. Once the territory is established they may advertise their presence to passing females through song. This is given from high exposed perches, and the song is

A male eastern bluebird perched at the nest entrance while the female looks on — typical bluebird courtship behavior.

generally quite loud. Song may be given as often as 25 times per minute. While singing, the male looks in all directions, possibly for females. He then will usually fly high in the air while moving to other perches about his territory. Song is often given while making these flights.

Courtship Displays

Once a female arrives on the territory, the male's behavior changes markedly. At this time he sings only occasionally, usually from low perches, and often very softly so that it is not easily heard from over 25 yards away.

He will also start a variety of other behaviors and displays that seem to call attention to the various nest holes on his territory. These same behaviors will be seen right away in the male if the pair arrive together on the territory.

For example, using the flight display, which is a slow, stalling flight, the male will fly to a nest box, then cling to the entrance. While at the entrance he may repeatedly poke his head in and out or cling there and do the wing-wave display, flicking open one or both wings at a moderate speed.

The female may follow him and perch on top of the box or at the entrance. If she does not go in, then the male may continue his actions or do a flight display to another box and try to interest her in that one. In addition, he might bring bits of nesting material in his beak to the box entrance. He may also enter and leave repeatedly or repeatedly hover in front of the box entrance.

Generally, when you see both birds go into a nest box together several times, that means that the two are paired and that they are likely to use that box as a nest site.

Courtship and nest box selection can take several days. So if at first a little occurs on one day

A male and female eastern bluebird pair, already attached to a nest box and ready to breed.

and then the birds fly off, do not worry. They may return again that day, the next day, or several days later. Previously paired birds or experienced birds usually go through this process more rapidly. Inexperienced birds may seem tentative in their commitment to each other and a nest site.

Actions of the Pair

Once two bluebirds are paired you will again begin to see different behaviors. One is termed mate-feeding, in which the male gets food and feeds it to the female. Sometimes she may crouch and wing-wave as she receives the food. Mate-feeding continues from the start of pairing on into the nestling phase. How much it occurs varies with individuals.

As the pair fly about the territory, they tend to keep in touch with calls and visual displays. A short call may be one of the ways the pair stay in contact when they cannot see each other. And the wing-wave display may be done by one or both birds as they come together after being apart.

The male will follow the female closely as she

forages or builds the nest. In most cases he will be present as she leaves or enters the nest hole, and he may actually signal her to come off the nest by wing-wave, calls, or having food to feed her. This close following continues from the beginning of pairing into the nestling phase.

Two reasons have been suggested for this behavior. One is that he is preventing her from mating with other males. Another is that his signaling her to come off the nest allows him to see first if the "coast is clear," and to make sure there are no hawks or other dangers that she cannot see from the nest entrance.

Another behavior of the pair that you may see is the male's chasing the female for short distances. These chases look aggressive but they seem to stimulate the female rather than deter her from her activities. For example, we once observed a female eastern bluebird that was very slow at building the nest. Several times the male dove at her and chased her, and after each of these incidents she increased her nest-building activity.

Copulation

Bluebirds can be seen copulating from the beginning of nest building until the start of incubation. Copulation can occur several times during this period. It is believed that among many small birds, such as the bluebird, fertilization is most effective about 4 days before an egg is laid.

Copulation usually occurs within 30 feet of the nest and may occur on top of the nest box. During copulation, the female crouches down, may quiver her wings, and lifts her tail up. The male lands on her back and bends his tail down to make contact and transfer sperm. The external sexual organs of most birds are alike in male and female and are simply openings called cloacas.

Studies of bluebird nestlings have shown that their parents are not always the adults that are attending the nest. This means either that the female mated with another male and then laid the resulting egg in the nest, or that another female laid the egg in the nest when the original female was not around. This latter behavior is called egg dumping; for more on this, see page 75.

When either the male or female mates with another bluebird, this is called an extra-pair copulation. This clearly occurs in bluebirds. One of the ways members of a pair prevent this is by chasing other bluebirds of the same sex out of the territory.

Interestingly, as noted, intruding males often drop down from high in the sky and land near the nest. This may be to optimize their chances of mating with the resident female, since copulations take place near the nest. When a resident male discovers another male near the nest box, he not only chases him away but may then copulate with his mate. This is believed to dilute the sperm possibly left by the intruding male.

Polygamy Versus Monogamy

There are many reported instances of one male bluebird having two females in the same territory, both females having nest boxes and being fed by the male. There are also known cases in which two males have attended one female and raised two successful broods in this manner. In addition, there have been reports of two females raising young in the same box with one male.

Traditionally, the bluebird has been seen as monogamous, but these examples seem to suggest that it can at times be polygamous. Then again, once you realize that extra-pair copulations are occurring and that the young in a nest can be from several different parents, then the definitions of polygamy and monogamy as applied to bluebirds become unclear.

Bluebirds are usually *apparently* monogamous; at least their obvious social relationships around the nest are monogamous. But genetically, all kinds of amazing mixing is going on.

Renestings, Second Broods, Lost Mates

When a nesting fails for one or more of a variety of reasons, bluebirds will try to renest. In most cases they leave the old nest and try a new one. In some cases they may move to a new territory, and in other cases they may even attempt to find new mates.

All three species of bluebirds can have two broods and in some cases up to three broods a

A male eastern bluebird perched at the entrance to a perfect natural nest cavity.

year. Second broods are usually with the same mate and on the same territory, possibly even in the same nest box. In some cases, however, a male or female may find a new mate for a second brood. In any case, there will be a renewal of some of the courtship displays at the start of additional broods.

Pairs that breed successfully in one year may stay together in following years, until one member dies. If a male loses a mate during the nesting season, then he will renew singing from exposed perches in order to attract a new one. There have been cases in which one male has had three different mates in a single season, because of predation on the first two.

When a female loses her mate, then she is more likely to leave the area and search for another male.

Differences Between the Species

Courtship in mountain and western bluebirds has yet to be closely studied and written about. Courtship among western bluebirds can include allopreening, in which mates peck lightly at each other's heads before copulating. In general, the courtship behavior of all three species seems quite similar. This may be one of the reasons that mixed pairs and hybrids occur as frequently as they do.

NEST BUILDING

Nest Location

Bluebirds, as secondary cavity nesters, cannot excavate their own cavity in trees, but must find one already made. In the wild, these tree cavities are either rotted-out holes or holes excavated by primary cavity nesters, such as woodpeckers. Although woodpeckers nest throughout wooded areas, bluebirds tend to choose holes that are near the kind of open areas in which they like to feed.

An eastern bluebird nest made with pine needles and containing 4 eggs.

Before humans offered nest boxes, bluebirds did not have a lot of choice about the location of their nests; they had to use what was available. In one study of natural nest sites of the mountain bluebird in Oregon, 18 nests in tree cavities were located. They were all in evergreens. The majority were in dead snags of ponderosa pine; 14 of the 18 had been excavated by common flickers; and the average height was 19 feet above ground.

Today, one of the main places that bluebirds nest is in nest boxes. These mimic the natural cavities and in some ways can be improvements upon them. They are usually better situated, have entrance holes that exclude certain other bird competitors, and they are generally drier and better ventilated.

In addition to these two choices, bluebirds have been known to nest in a variety of other locations. When wooden fence posts were common and trees were cleared from land, woodpeckers often hollowed out cavities in the posts. Afterward, these became good places for bluebirds to nest. This is particularly true of the western and eastern bluebirds, which typically nest in low-lying farmlands.

There is also a long list of unusual bluebird nest sites. In strip-mined areas, eastern bluebirds have used crevices between rocks or protected niches in banks. Eastern bluebirds have also nested in the ends of stacked drainpipes, holes in clay banks, old mailboxes, cliff swallow nests, the barrel of a cannon, and on top of an old barn swallow nest near the light fixture of a garage.

Western bluebirds have nested in the mud nests of cliff swallows and in crevices in buildings. Mountain bluebirds have been seen nesting in cliff swallow nests, old robin nests, on top of rafters inside buildings, in outbuildings, stone fences, mailboxes, pipes, and storage boxes.

Nest Building

Although the male may take the lead in exploring nest boxes and trying to draw the female to certain sites, it is the female who makes the final choice of where the nest is built. This choosing can be done in a day, or it may take weeks. Again, pairs that have bred in the area before are usually faster at selecting a site; inexperienced pairs are often slower.

The female is also the one that does all of the actual nest building. Males may carry nesting material during courtship, and a little later they may carry bits of it again, possibly to stimulate the female, but this never amounts to much real building. While the female is building, the male may even enter the nest and remove a stray bit of material. Why he does this is not known.

A nest can be completed in just 2 days but on average takes 4–5 days. In some cases, especially early in the season, nest building may start and stop over a 6-week period. Thus, when you see nest building, do not be surprised if the birds leave and then come back, if they start to build a little in several boxes, or if they take a particularly long time. All of these patterns and more are just part of the tremendous variation in individual bluebird habits.

Bluebird nests are constructed of grasses, pine needles, fine weed stalks, and occasionally fine rootlets. The female gathers bits of the material, flies to the box, and arranges it inside. To form the hollow in the nest, she will sit inside it and press her breast up against the sides. This is called molding.

Bluebird nests are airy and light but well-built, and have a small, neat cup shape in the center. The center may be lined with finer grasses or rarely just a few bits of hair or feathers.

Second broods or second attempts can occur in the same nest box; a new nest is just built on top of the old one. Sometimes old material from the previous nest is removed by the birds, but they will not try to remove the whole nest. If you are monitoring the boxes, it is best to remove all nesting material after the young have fledged or immediately after a failed nesting attempt. This keeps the nest box clean and allows the new nest to be the proper height from the entrance hole.

A female eastern bluebird at the nest box with a beakful of building material.

Bluebirds usually spend less time building nests for their second and third broods.

Sometimes you will see bluebirds carrying nesting material to nest boxes in fall. This does not result in a completed nest. Why they do this is not known; it does not seem to be related to whether they will use the box for roosting that winter, or for breeding the following spring.

Encouraging Nest Building

Sometimes a female may seem reluctant to build. In this case, there are several things you can do that may encourage her. One is to gather dry, fine grasses or pine needles and place them in little bunches in the general area of the nest or beneath perches where the birds often land. We have done this with our bluebirds, and the females have gone to them within minutes.

Other people have had some success with placing a few strands of material in the nest hole. This may help to stimulate the female.

An eastern bluebird nest made with fine grasses, bits of fur, and a feather.

Species Differences

It is generally the case that only the female builds the nest, but there are a few accounts of both male and female western bluebirds building the nest.

The eastern bluebird usually uses just grasses or pine needles in its nest, with only rarely a lining that might include feathers. In one case, a female eastern bluebird was assisted by two juvenile bluebirds as she built her nest. They may have been her young from the previous brood.

Among mountain bluebirds, when the male removes bits of nesting material, this often results in a short flurry of increased building by the female. She may start to make trips for material about every 2 minutes. Mountain bluebirds take 11–14 days to complete first-brood nests and only 4–5 days to complete second-brood nests.

Mountain bluebirds often use shreds of sage or aspen bark that the female pulls off the plants; occasionally there are even shreds of plastic in the nest. Mountain bluebirds may also switch boxes while nest building; one pair were seen building to some extent in three different boxes at the same time.

Western bluebirds also occasionally use feathers in their nests and build in more than one nest box.

A male eastern bluebird at a natural cavity that has resulted from rotting. It is removing the fecal sac of one of the nestlings inside.

EGG LAYING

Egg Laying

Once the nest is completed, egg laying can begin. In general, it starts within a day or two of nest completion, but there can be as much as a week or more before it starts. During this time, you may not see the birds around the nest. In fact, they may appear to have deserted it.

Eggs are generally laid in the morning. We have discovered eggs laid as early as 7:00 A.M. and as late as 9:30 A.M. The actual laying of the egg can be done within a few minutes. Usually one egg is laid each day until the clutch is complete, although sometimes there may be an extra day in the middle when no egg is laid. This happened to one of our bluebirds on a particularly cold and rainy day.

Bluebirds, like many other songbirds, do not spend a lot of time around the nest during egg laying. Rather, the female will be out feeding and the male will be closely following her. During this time you may see copulation; it usually occurs near the nest.

Occasionally during egg laying, the female will remain on the nest for periods of up to 30 minutes, but she is not actually incubating the eggs. Why she does this is not known. The eggs will not be incubated at night either. They remain at the same temperature as the air, usually with no harm. They are able to stay in this static state until all the eggs are laid and incubation begins.

The timing of the first clutch can vary tremendously from year to year. For example, one year at an eastern bluebird trail in the Midwest, the first egg was laid as early as March 26; another year the first egg was not laid until early June. This variability is usually due to the weather. Warm weather encourages earlier egg laying; cold weather and snows can delay it. Mountain bluebirds are less affected by cold weather in early spring and may start egg laying when temperatures are below freezing and may be incubating during snowstorms.

Clutch Sizes for Each Species

Mountain bluebird clutches for first broods can have as many as 8 eggs. But generally only about 3 percent of mountain bluebird clutches have more than 6 eggs. Their average clutch size is 4, 5, or 6 eggs.

Four blue eggs in an eastern bluebird nest.

When Are Eggs Laid?

When you are trying to attract nesting bluebirds, it is important to know when the nesting season starts and ends. Here are some samples for each species of *early* dates when eggs have been found in certain regions of the continent:

Eastern Bluebird
In the South — late March
In the middle latitudes — early April
In the North — mid-April

Mountain Bluebird
In the South — early April
In the middle latitudes — mid-April
In the North — late April

Western Bluebird
In the South — late March
In the middle latitudes — early April
In the North — late-April

Since bluebirds can have up to three broods per season, you can still find eggs of all three species being laid in late July. It is a long season, with many chances to attract successful breeding pairs to your area. So keep your hopes up.

An unusual shot of an eastern female passing a defective egg out of the nest to the male.

Additional Broods

Bluebirds, under good conditions, can usually have two broods in a season. With a warm spring and an early first brood, they can even have three broods in one summer. Events that interfere with the process of successive broods include bad weather, especially early in the season, parasites in the nest, predators, and competition from other cavity-nesting birds.

Clutches for second broods are usually smaller than clutches for first broods, often by one egg. Why this occurs is not known, but it may have to do with the physical demands on the female for egg production while she is still feeding fledglings from a previous brood.

Infertile Eggs

It is often the case that some eggs in a clutch do not hatch. In about 10–15 percent of bluebird eggs, the embryos never start to develop. These eggs are termed infertile. Infertility can be caused by several factors, including a defect in the sexual organs of the male or female, the ingestion of chemicals that may make one or both members of a pair sterile, and temporary malnutrition of the female during egg production.

Eastern bluebird clutches for first broods are most commonly 3, 4, or 5 eggs, although sometimes 6-egg clutches can occur. Eastern bluebird clutches range from 1 to 6 eggs, and, rarely, 7 eggs.

Western bluebird clutches for first broods are usually 5–6 eggs. But it is not uncommon for them to have up to 8 eggs in a clutch.

Occasionally, nests of any of the three species have an abnormally large number of eggs, such as the nest of a mountain bluebird that contained 10 eggs. Large clutches such as this may be the result of egg dumping, or possibly the laying of a second clutch over a failed first clutch. This latter behavior was seen in an eastern bluebird that laid 4 new eggs over 3 infertile eggs and sat on all 7 during incubation.

Other eggs may be fertile but for some reason stop developing during incubation. This arrested development could be caused by a defect in the embryo or possibly by overexposure to heat or cold at some point during incubation.

Female bluebirds vary in their response to eggs that will not hatch. In some cases they seem to abandon a clutch after 4 or 5 days of incubating. How they determine that the eggs will not hatch is not known. In other cases, they may incubate them for twice the normal length (which ranges from 12 to 18 days) before giving up. In one extreme case, a female eastern bluebird incubated a clutch for 84 days — about six times the normal duration — before giving up.

Once the birds decide the eggs should not be incubated anymore, they may act in one of several ways. Some females build a new nest right over the old eggs and lay a new clutch. Others move to new boxes before renesting.

In clutches with some normal eggs and one or more infertile ones, the female raises the healthy young when they hatch. The unhatched egg may be left in the nest throughout the nestling phase, or the parents may try to remove it.

Variation in Eggs

As you monitor bluebird nests, you are likely to come across eggs that vary from the norm either in color or size. The normal color of bluebird eggs is a rich sky blue, but sometimes you will find eggs that are light blue or even white. Eggs of the mountain bluebird are a slightly lighter color generally than those of the eastern and western bluebirds.

White eggs are called albanistic eggs. It is not known why they occur. In general a female will lay all white or all blue eggs in a clutch, not some of one and some of the other. However, sometimes clutches are found with just one white egg and the rest normal blue. This is probably a result of egg dumping.

Albanistic eggs have been found in nests of all three species of bluebirds. In general, their hatching success is the same as that of other, normally colored eggs. One western bluebird female is known to have laid three clutches of all albanistic eggs and all were fertile. Another study of mountain bluebird eggs showed that 2–3 percent of all eggs were pale blue and 3–4 percent were albanistic. In this study, pale blue and white eggs ac-

A clutch of white eggs in a western bluebird nest. The pencil is in the picture for scale.

tually had a higher percent chance of hatching than normal blue eggs. A study of eastern bluebird eggs showed that over 9 percent were white and all hatched at a high rate.

There is no known connection between albanistic eggs and albino birds; normally colored birds can hatch from albanistic eggs and albino birds from blue eggs.

Another variation that you may witness is eggs that are substantially smaller than the norm. These are sometimes referred to as dwarf, or runt, eggs, and they are not fully developed inside, sometimes having no yolk. They are usually infertile, and it is not yet known what causes them.

Normal variation in egg sizes within a clutch can also occur. One study of the eastern bluebird found that egg size increased slightly as egg laying progressed, the last egg being the largest.

Egg Dumping

It has recently been discovered that bluebird mating systems are more complicated than had previously been thought. Although, for the most part, bluebirds seem to be monogamous, studies show that up to 9 percent of nests have one or more young with at least one parent that is different from the two that are caring for it.

This can result in two ways. An intruding male can come into the territory and mate with the resident female so that at least one of her eggs has a different father. Or a female can intrude onto the territory and lay her egg in the resident female's nest. She may have mated with the resident male or another male. This behavior — one female's laying an egg in the nest of another bird — is called egg dumping.

Brown-headed cowbirds lay their eggs in the nests of other species, and this is called *inter*specific egg dumping. Cowbirds have been known to egg dump in the nests of all three species of bluebirds. They enter the nest cavity when the pair are not around and within seconds can lay an egg in the nest. In some cases the bluebird pair attending the nest end up raising the cowbird along with their own young. In other cases they may abandon the nest and renest elsewhere.

A female eastern bluebird poised on the front of a nest box.

Bluebirds egg dump in their own species' nests, and this is called *intra*specific egg dumping. This may be the cause of unusually large clutches, since the egg dumper has added another egg. It also may be the cause of cases in which one egg in a clutch is very different from the others, such as one albanistic egg in a clutch of otherwise all-blue eggs. It may even be the cause of one infertile egg's being in a nest of otherwise fertile eggs.

INCUBATION

When Does Incubation Start?

During egg laying, the female leaves the eggs unattended and will not start incubating them until the last egg is laid, although on rare occasions she may start incubating with the laying of the next to last egg. If you have occasion to touch the eggs while monitoring during this stage, you can feel that they are cold. Obviously, the first egg laid remains the longest in this state, up to 8 days in large clutches of western or mountain bluebirds. During this time the eggs are able to remain in a suspended state; growth is then restarted when the female begins incubating.

Once incubation starts, the eggs are kept warm all the time. They must be warmed to at least 95°F to develop properly. The female's body is at about 106°F, and by making direct contact with the eggs she can easily warm them to the required temperature. It is believed that if the eggs get warmer than about 107°F because of overheating in the nest box, they may die. This is why nest box ventilation is important.

There are several theories on why the female

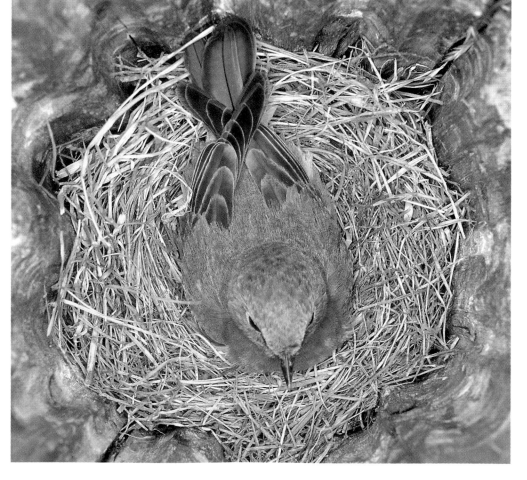

A female eastern bluebird incubating eggs.

A male eastern bluebird bringing food to the nest for his incubating female.

waits until the last egg is laid to start incubation. One involves the difficulty of doing two different activities at once. If she started incubating after the first egg was laid, when that egg hatched she would need to feed that nestling and incubate the other eggs at the same time. Also, the firstborn would fledge earlier, and the parents would have to divide their time between trips to the nest and tracking down a wandering fledgling to feed it.

Another reason for delaying the start of incubation could be that early-hatching nestlings crowd out their younger siblings and get more of the food, thus hurting the chances of the younger birds' normal growth.

Who Incubates

Among most songbirds, incubation is done by the female. This is also the case with all three species of bluebirds. The female develops what is called a brood patch. This is an area on the breast of the bird where the down feathers are lost just prior to incubation and where an increased number of blood vessels develop. By the time the young have fledged, the skin has returned to normal. If a second or third brood occurs, the development of blood vessels starts all over again.

The male bluebird may enter the box when the female is out and may sit over the eggs, but because he does not have a brood patch, he cannot warm the eggs to the temperature at which they will be actively developing.

A male mountain bluebird feeding and watching over his nest site during the incubation phase.

Behavior During Incubation

During incubation the female sits almost constantly over the eggs, exposing them to the full warmth of her brood patch. She incubates the eggs for one continuous period during the night and during the day does shorter stretches, periodically leaving the nest to preen and feed. On hot days she may leave the eggs unattended for longer periods of time.

In many cases the male may come to the nest or land nearby and sing, wing-wave, or bring food. This may in fact be a signal that all is clear and it is safe for her to leave.

While the female is away, the male generally remains near the box and may even go inside. However, he does not spread his wings out over the eggs as if incubating. The male mountain bluebird is known to poke at the nest and possibly remove grass bits during these visits. When the female returns he will leave. At night, the male may stay in the box with the female, sitting on the rim of the nest while the female incubates.

The female, before settling on the eggs again after being away, may gently turn the eggs with her bill. This is believed to help the eggs get evenly warmed and to keep the inner membrane of the egg from sticking to the shell.

Bluebirds are also known for a curious behavior in which they poke their bill down into the nesting material and rapidly vibrate it for a few seconds. This has been termed tremble-thrust. It occurs throughout the incubation and nestling phases. Its function is not known for sure, but it may help to adjust nesting material, or it may shake parasites, such as blowfly larvae, down to the bottom of the nest.

Length of Incubation

The length of incubation varies with the species, the behavior of the pair, and the weather. Average incubation time for eastern bluebirds is 12–14 days (range 12–18 days), for mountain bluebirds 13–15 days (range 12–16 days), and for western bluebirds 14 days (range 13–17 days).

The times the female is on the nest are called attentive periods, and times when she is off are inattentive periods. In a study of the mountain bluebird, average attentive periods during the

A female mountain bluebird during one of her attentive periods on the nest.

day were 25–34 minutes and average inattentive periods were 4–7 minutes. One particularly long attentive period was more than 2½ hours.

The length of the female's daytime attentive periods may be influenced by the number of times the male feeds her. It was discovered in this study that with just one feeding, she stayed on the nest for 25 minutes, with two feedings she stayed for 41 minutes, and with three or more feedings, she stayed on the nest for an average of 78 minutes. Thus, with a male feeding the female more, she may be able to incubate more constantly, and this may shorten the length of incubation.

Weather also affects the length of incubation. Cold weather can slow the development of the eggs and also make it harder for the female to find food, which means that the eggs are exposed for longer periods and to colder temperatures. In one case, the incubation period for an eastern bluebird was 21 days during very cold weather.

The eggs can withstand some cooling for brief periods of time.

In warmer areas of the continent, heat may cause some eggs to start developing even without the female's being there. Or it may shorten incubation periods by a day or so, whether the female is on the nest or not. Generally, in hot weather, the female has longer inattentive periods. She seems to know instinctively how much warming the eggs need.

NESTLINGS

Hatching

The eggs hatch over a period of a day or more and usually in the order in which they were laid. In very warm weather, eggs laid early may start development before incubation begins and hatch several days ahead of the others.

The young break out of the egg with the aid of an "egg-tooth," a hardening at the tip of their upper bill designed just for this purpose. Once the young hatch, the egg-tooth is reabsorbed into the bird's body and disappears.

When you find a piece of eggshell on the ground or in a nest, you can tell if the egg was preyed upon or hatched. Eggs that have hatched have at least a partial straight line of broken shell at the largest diameter of the egg. This is due to the actions of the young bird pecking its way out. A shell broken completely irregularly, or just punctured, is more likely the result of predation. After the eggs hatch, the female may remove the eggshells or partially eat them, since they contain nutrients such as calcium.

Behavior of the Adults

During the first few days after hatching, the female may remain on the nest almost to the extent that she did during incubation. At this point her sitting over the young is called brooding, and its purpose is to keep the young warm. How much brooding she does depends on the weather. In warmer weather the young can be left unattended for longer periods; when it is colder she may need to stay over them almost constantly.

The male may bring food to the nest; the female eats some and feeds the rest to the nestlings. Depending on the temperature, she may get off the nest and collect additional food for the young. The parents tend to feed each young an average of two times per hour, no matter what the size of the brood.

Among western bluebirds, the male continues to bring food to the young birds at the same rate throughout the nestling phase, while the female's visits tend to increase in frequency to the point that they outnumber those of the male. In one study of eastern bluebirds, a different pattern occurred — over the nestling phase, male visits decreased while female visits increased.

A pair of eastern bluebirds at their nest box, the male at the entrance with food for the nestlings and the female perched above, supervising.

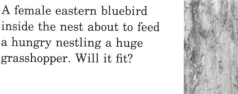

A female eastern bluebird inside the nest about to feed a hungry nestling a huge grasshopper. Will it fit?

Another study of eastern bluebirds compared the success after egg laying of lone females to females with mates; it was found that in both groups there was equal success in raising young to the fledgling stage, suggesting that in this species, male parental care is not a necessity. However, in this study, the fledgling phase was not watched, and this may be the one that puts the most pressure on adults to find food for their young.

You can estimate the age of the nestlings by watching the feeding behavior of the adults. If when the parents bring food to the nest, they go all the way in and do not leave with fecal sacs (see below), the young are probably 1–5 days old. If the parents go all the way into the nest to feed the young and leave with a fecal sac, then the nestlings are about 6–12 days old. If the parents just dip their heads into the entrance hole to feed the young, then they are probably 12–18 days old.

Nest Sanitation

You may see one of the adults leave the nest with a white blob in its bill. This is a fecal sac — the droppings of one of the young all contained in a little membrane. Removal by adults is the way the nest is kept clean. Up to about the fifth to seventh day of nestling life the parents may eat the fecal sacs; after this they carry them off and drop them away from the nest. Sometimes fecal sacs are all dropped at a certain spot, such as the top of a fence post, and will accumulate there until washed away by rains.

Bluebird nests are often clean of feces right through the nestling phase. This is especially true of eastern and western bluebirds. Among mountain bluebirds and some other birds, such as tree swallows, droppings begin to accumulate in the nest during the days just prior to fledging, resulting in a messy nest by the time they leave.

Development and Behavior of the Young

When the young first hatch they do not look at all like birds. Their eyes are closed, they have no feathers except a few traces of down, and they can barely move except to lift their heads slightly and, of course, open their mouths. Because they have no feathers, they cannot regulate their body temperature; this is why the female must brood them until their feathers develop enough to hold

Hatching Day–Day 1: One young has just hatched. The down on its back looks like dark lines because it is still wet and stuck together.

About Day 4: Dark areas on wings and head are where feathers are beginning to develop just under the skin. (The adult male is removing a fecal sac.)

in the warmth. Western bluebirds take about 8 days to do this, mountain bluebirds about 6 days, and eastern bluebirds about 5 days. Once they have feathers, keeping warm is just a matter of getting enough food.

The period just after the female has stopped brooding can still be a critical stage for the nestlings. If the weather is very cold and wet, the young may get so chilled that they do not respond by lifting their heads up when the parents arrive with food. In these cases, the parents may stop feeding the young, and the young may die. (See Monitoring Bluebird Boxes, page 42.)

At first the young are fed small, soft foods, such as caterpillars or spiders. Later they are fed larger insects, such as grasshoppers and ground beetles, and if there are ripe berries around, these may also be added to the diet of the young.

As you monitor the nest, you will see the young nestlings at various stages of their growth. To help you to estimate how old they are, we have provided a brief field guide to their age in this chapter. You need to know their age in order not to cause them to leave the nest prematurely by

monitoring at the wrong time. (See Monitoring Bluebird Boxes.)

Helpers at the Nest

Many bluebirders have noticed extra birds associated with a breeding pair and helping them to raise their young.

Rarely, this type of behavior can involve two different species. This usually occurs when two species are nesting near each other or when a bird loses its young and others in the same stage of breeding are nearby. For example, a male pygmy nuthatch nesting in a natural cavity just 20 inches away from a mountain bluebird nest started to feed the nestling bluebirds while his mate was still incubating eggs. The bluebirds showed very little aggression toward him, and he continued to pay attention to the bluebird young even when his own young hatched.

In another case, a bluebird fed some chickadees. The two species were nesting in boxes 40 feet apart. The chickadees hatched before the bluebirds, and during the last few days of their

About Day 6: Feathers are just beginning to break through the skin on the head and wings of these nestlings.

About Day 9: Eyes are open and feathers are breaking out of their sheaths.

A Field Guide to Estimating the Age of Nestling Bluebirds

Determining the age of nestlings is not an exact science, since a great deal of variation occurs among nestlings of a single brood and among different broods. The speed of development is also dependent on the species, the weather, the amount of food available, and the number of birds feeding the young. Nevertheless, here are some clues that will help you estimate the age of nestlings. *Once nestling eastern bluebirds are 12 days old and mountain or western bluebirds 14 days old, the nest box should not be opened,* for disturbance at this time may cause the young to leave the nest prematurely, and this greatly hinders their chances of survival.

Hatching Day–Day 1
Birds one to two times the size of the egg. Sparse black down, mostly on the head and a little on the spine. Eyes closed.

Day 2–Day 4
Body weight has more than doubled since Day 1. Eyes closed. By Day 4, feathers begin to develop under the skin and appear as small dark areas along the wings and dark areas on the head, partially obscured by the down.

Day 5–Day 7
Feathers begin to break through the skin on the wings and the back of the head. Outer portion of wings is all dark due to feather development. By Day 7, feathers start to open out of their sheaths. Eyes are open as slits.

Day 8–Day 11
Eyes are all the way open. The primary feathers of the wings continue to unsheathe. Birds may preen slightly. Birds have more than three-quarters their final body weight, and most further growth is in the form of feather development. You may be able to determine the sex of the birds on their 11th day by looking at their wing feathers. Those of the male will be bright blue, while those of the female will be paler gray-blue.

Day 12–Day 19
Birds are physically active in the nest. They can exercise their wings, stretch, and preen. The white ring around the eye becomes noticeable.

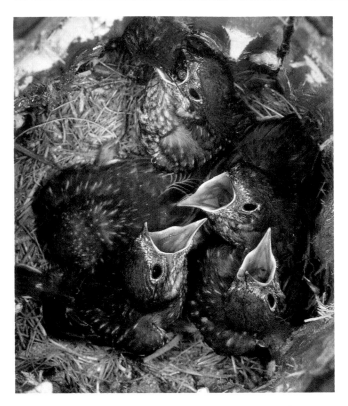

About Day 16: Birds are physically active and white eye-ring is distinct.

nestling life the male bluebird started to feed them. The chickadees were excited when he first entered the nest. The bluebird continued feeding the nestlings until they fledged a few days later. He even seemed to protect the box against other birds and a squirrel. A few days later, his own young hatched and he fed them.

More commonly, bluebird young help feed subsequent broods of their parents. For example, while a mother eastern bluebird was incubating her second brood, two young from the first brood were being fed by the father. When the second brood hatched, the young from the first brood followed the parents as they collected food and even entered the box and fed the nestlings.

Sometimes the behavior of these young helpers is not as clear and direct as that of the parents. In one case, two juvenile birds just sat on the box as the parents repeatedly made food trips to their second-brood nestlings. A few days later, the juveniles were seen with food in their bills. They would land on the box, flutter along the side as if looking for the entrance, and even enter and leave the box still holding the food. Finally, they made trips into the box and came out without the food. In this example, the helpers did not remove fecal sacs.

Another observation of the eastern bluebird showed that a male bred successfully in his first year about a mile from his parents. After finishing his first brood, he flew to his parents' territory with his two young, but not his mate, and assisted his parents in feeding the young from their second brood. The young from the parents' first brood also helped them feed the young through the nestling phases. The adult male and his first-year son continued to feed the young through the fledgling phase.

The young who help out at the nest benefit in several ways: they improve their foraging ability, gain experience feeding young, are allowed to stay in the family area (young of many other species of songbirds are kicked out), and enhance their safety, since there are more birds to detect danger.

There are also advantages for the parents. One is that their offspring benefit and will in turn become more successful parents. In addition, having help means they can raise more young in the second brood. In general, nests attended by helpers have a higher success rate. Help may even shorten the nestling period, possibly leaving enough time for a third brood.

Violet-Green Swallows and Western Bluebirds

In the process of studying western bluebirds, one researcher saw three instances of violet-green swallows' helping the bluebirds raise their young in the later nestling stages. The violet-green swallows, which also use nest boxes, defended the nest site, removed fecal sacs, and fed the young. The swallows defended the boxes from tree swallows and violet-green swallows, and one often sat in the box with its head out the entrance while the bluebirds were away foraging. There were even times when a swallow and an adult bluebird were in the nest together.

The survival rate in these swallow-assisted boxes was higher than in unassisted western bluebird nests. In two cases, the swallows went

A male eastern bluebird looking over his nestlings after feeding them.

on to use the nest box when the bluebirds were finished.

Why this cooperation occurred is open to speculation. It is possible that while helping the bluebirds, the swallows established territorial rights to the box against other swallows and that they got full access to the box by assuring a swift and successful brood of the bluebirds. There clearly needs to be more study of this fascinating relationship between the two species.

Length of Nestling Phase

The length of the nestling phase can vary. For the eastern bluebird, the range is from 16 to 21 days. For the mountain bluebird, this phase ranges from 19 to 23 days. And for the western bluebird the nestling phase is from 19 to 22 days.

The shorter nestling phases may result from a variety of factors, including warmer weather, an abundance of prey near the nest, helpers at the nest, or trail monitors who provide extra food in the form of mealworms. The longer nestling phases can result from lack of food or inclement weather.

FLEDGLINGS

What Is a Fledgling?

A fledgling is a bird that is out of the nest but still dependent on its parents for food. We sometimes jokingly refer to this stage as "college age." Once the fledgling bluebirds can gather food on their own, they are termed juvenile birds, for they still have their juvenal plumage. When these birds molt into adult plumage in fall, they are called adults.

Leaving the Nest

Nestling bluebirds instinctively know when to leave the nest. They become increasingly restless at the end of the nestling stage, moving about and stretching their wings. On the day of leaving, the parents may call from outside the nest and may not bring as much food, possibly as a kind of encouragement to fledge.

Adult bluebirds do not have to teach the young how to fly; they can fly instinctively. Their first flight can carry them 100 feet from the nest and in one reported case, 450 feet. They usually head for the nearest perch. This is why it is helpful if a bluebird box is placed so that it faces a nearby tree or shrub where the fledglings can make their first landing.

Usually all of the young leave the nest within an hour or two on the same day, but occasionally some nestlings remain until the next day. Once the young have left the nest, they never again return that summer.

Sometimes nestlings leave the nest before they are ready. This usually occurs when a predator threatens the nest. For example, a snake near an eastern bluebird nest caused the parents to give an alarm call, which in turn made the young jump from the nest cavity. In this instance, jumping out was safer than staying in the nest. Out of the nest, the young could hop into bushes for safety and the parents would feed them there.

Fledgling Behavior

A fledgling's main concerns are safety and getting fed. For safety, a fledgling generally moves to treetops, well away from ground predators and where it can see for a distance.

In contrast to the situation when it was in the nest, the fledgling now needs to make its whereabouts known to the parents in order to be fed. After gathering food, the parents return to the general area of the young and then must find the specific location of each one. To aid them, the fledglings generally give a plaintive call at frequent regular intervals. However, a parent's warning call may make them stop momentarily. It also behooves the fledglings to stay together, since this gives them more eyes to spot danger and parents approaching with food, and some assurance that they will not be aced out of a feeding by one of their siblings.

Thus, fledglings generally just sit in one place and call. They may also huddle together at night or during the day, possibly for increased warmth. They can look very forlorn at this stage and sometimes seem abandoned, since intervals between feedings can be long. But you must resist the urge to help them in any way at this stage, for in the majority of cases they are being well cared for by their parents.

Often the parents may lead the young to an area away from the nest for a time, possibly to a spot where there is greater safety or a greater abundance of food. Their trips from food to young are thus shortened, and they can better look out for their safety. Because of this, you may have difficulty locating a family of bluebirds once the young have fledged.

A fledgling bluebird looking for its next good perch.

A Helping Hand — Or Beak

Which parent feeds the fledglings varies with each brood and with individual pairs. In some cases, both parents participate. In other cases, just the male may feed the fledglings while the female starts building the nest and laying the eggs for a second or third brood. In one case, a male eastern bluebird was known to feed his own fledglings by himself and also those from a neighboring territory whose mother had disappeared and whose father had remated with another female. This one male took care of 7 fledglings in all.

In many other cases during second and third broods, fledglings are fed by juvenile birds from the earlier broods. Sometimes these helpers can even be adult birds that were born to the same parents the previous year.

No More Free Lunch

By the second week, the fledglings begin to follow the parents about. This may assure that they get fed more often. It also may give them experience in where to look for food. After 3 weeks, the fledglings begin to gather some food on their own. This is done mostly by gleaning insects from perches or by picking them up while hopping along the ground. After the fourth week, the fledglings develop the typical bluebird feeding behavior of dropping to the ground after spotting an insect from a perch. In about their fifth week the young may be able to catch insects out of the air or by hovering and then dropping down.

Starting in the fourth or fifth week, the parents gradually stop feeding the young. Finally, after a fledgling phase of about 5 weeks, the young are on their own.

Life After Fledging

Juvenile birds often remain with their parents, or in the general vicinity of their territory, throughout summer and into fall. Occasionally, families of bluebirds will return to their nest cavity in fall for a day or so, often entering the nest briefly, or even bringing in a few strands of nesting material. Why they do this is not known.

FALL AND WINTER BEHAVIOR

Family Flocks

In late summer, when breeding is over, a pair of bluebirds with various young from broods of that year may form a small flock and wander about together as they feed. Sometimes these groups explore boxes, perching on top and entering.

In fall this family may join with other bluebird families and form an even larger flock — 50–100 birds for mountain bluebirds. In the past, fall flocks of the eastern bluebird could be as large as 100 birds, but now it is more typical to see flocks of from 5 to 20 birds. In northern areas these flocks start migrating in October and November. In other areas, family units and the larger flocks may stay together all winter and during cold weather may even roost together. In some winter roost boxes, monitors have discovered eastern bluebirds that are siblings and sometimes these are joined by one of the parents.

In spring the flocks break up and the birds return to nesting areas or stay in new nesting areas that they may have encountered in their winter wanderings.

Feeding Behavior

Once bluebirds are finished breeding, they are no longer tied to their breeding site and wander freely in search of areas with plentiful food. Grasshoppers, crickets, and spiders, all of which are abundant in fall, remain the birds' food of choice until they are no longer available because of cold and snow. Even as it gets cold and snows start to cover the ground, the birds may seek out any exposed ground or south-facing slope where the ground temperature is warmer and more insects may be active.

When ground temperatures go below freezing and arthropods become less active, bluebirds switch to eating berries almost exclusively. The berries are swallowed whole and, because bluebirds cannot easily crack seeds in their bill or digest them, the seeds are regurgitated or voided in their feces.

One study of the winter food habits of eastern bluebirds in Tennessee showed that sumac berries made up 85–95 percent of what they ate. But it also showed that, compared with other fruits the birds ate, such as the berries of possum haw, flowering dogwood, Japanese honeysuckle, and bittersweet, sumac berries had the lowest caloric

A male eastern bluebird perched on a bent cattail in a winter swamp.

A male mountain bluebird looking for food at the edge of open water where the snow has melted.

content of them all. The bluebirds had to eat up to ten times as many sumac berries to get the same energy they would get from eating fruits from these other plants. Why were the bluebirds choosing sumac?

One possible reason is that mockingbirds in the area were defending winter territories containing the higher-calorie fruits and keeping bluebirds off. This suggests that sumacs were not necessarily bluebirds' favorite fruit, nor the best one for them, but were simply the one most readily available that no other birds were eating.

Another problem for wintering bluebirds is the hordes of starlings that roam the countryside looking for berries to eat. A large flock of starlings can descend on a flowering dogwood tree and eat all of its fruit within several minutes. Because of this, certain shrubs and trees are no longer dependable sources of winter food for bluebirds. This is another example of how the intro-

duction of the starling has adversely affected bluebirds.

One of the biggest threats to bluebirds in winter is freezing rains or heavy snows that coat all berries in a thick layer of ice. This makes it almost impossible for them to feed, and some birds in colder areas may have trouble surviving. In these cases, bluebirds may come to feeders and accept suet, suet mixtures, raisins, currants, dried fruits, and wild berries laid out for them.

Migration

Even though many bluebirds are banded by field researchers to assist in identifying birds and tracking their movements, not much is known about bluebird migration. There are several reasons for this. Most banding occurs at nest boxes and not on wintering grounds. Thus we know a lot about whether bluebirds return to breeding sites, but practically nothing about where they go in winter. Also, since bluebirds do not travel along the traditional migration routes of other birds, they are not caught as often in nets at banding stations; if they were we could track their movements. In addition, most bluebirds are banded as nestlings, and mortality is as high as 50 percent during the first three months after fledging.

We do know that each of the three bluebird species has a different migration behavior. Western bluebirds are the least migratory and do very little latitudinal (north-south) migration. They may show up in new areas during winter, but this is a result of their moving short distances to areas where there is abundant food. They also tend to move from higher to lower elevations and the milder weather associated with them.

In late fall, eastern bluebirds in the North begin to wander south; they spend the winter in the southern two-thirds of the species' summer range. They do not have any established migration routes. Rather, their migration involves drifting to new areas where food may be abundant and the climate milder. This drifting seems to be triggered by extreme cold and the lack of food.

Eastern bluebirds can winter farther north if food is abundant, but if this food is covered by ice or heavy snows, the birds can have trouble surviving. Planting shrubs and trees that have berries in winter is one way you can help bluebirds. See Landscaping for Bluebirds, page 32.

Recoveries of banded eastern bluebirds have revealed these movements in winter. In the East, eastern bluebirds from New York and Pennsylvania have been found in Florida; and birds from New Hampshire and Massachusetts have been found in Georgia and the Carolinas.

In the Midwest, eastern bluebirds moved from Ontario and the Great Lakes states to the Gulf states. And birds from the northern Midwest and midwestern Canada have flown to Texas, Oklahoma, and Nebraska for the winter.

The mountain bluebird is the most migratory of the three species, coming down from Alaska and Canada into the Lower 48. Mountain bluebirds in the southwestern mountains may move into Mexico for the winter.

Studies of banded mountain bluebirds have shown that birds from as far north as Manitoba can winter in Oklahoma and Texas and that mountain bluebirds from western Canada may also fly to winter in Texas and New Mexico.

There are reports of 300–400 mountain bluebirds flocking in mid-August before flying south. In the spring, mountain bluebirds may also migrate north in large flocks, seeking protection in river canyons during severe weather.

Roosting

One of the ways that bluebirds survive cold temperatures on winter nights is to use cavities or nest boxes for roosting. This is a common habit, even in southern states, and is another good reason to provide nest boxes all year.

Most nights, bluebirds just roost in a protected spot, such as under the eaves of outbuildings and porches. One person put up little ledges in the eaves of her porch after seeing bluebirds trying to roost there, and the bluebirds adopted these as their regular roosting spot. There are very few records of where bluebirds actually roost in the wild.

On colder nights, generally when the temperature is below freezing, bluebirds seek extra protection by roosting in a cavity. What kind of cavity they choose or prefer is still open to question. One study compared natural cavities to nest boxes and roosting boxes — large boxes with a hole at the bottom and perches inside near the top. In this study the birds preferred natural cavities first, then nest boxes, and never used roosting boxes.

Some people think that if the ventilation holes in nesting boxes are plugged up, the boxes will be warmer and more attractive to roosting bluebirds. One study compared "winterized" versus standard nest boxes and found that over the course of the winter, bluebirds used more of the winterized boxes as roosts.

More needs to be discovered about the conditions under which bluebirds are most likely to roost in cavities. In Georgia, eastern bluebirds were found to roost at any temperature under freezing. In a study in Tennessee, they did not seem to roost in boxes until the temperature was

At least 11, and possibly 12 or more, eastern bluebirds roosting in an artificially made cavity in a tree trunk.

below 14°F. In any case, as it gets colder more bluebirds are likely to roost in cavities. More birds are also likely to roost in cavities during January and February than during November and December.

Another interesting feature of bluebird roosting is that the birds tend to roost in groups. In one study of 102 boxes in Ohio, nine boxes were used during one 25°F night; the number of birds in these boxes was 1, 2, 2, 3, 3, 4, 4, 4, and 7, respectively. On particularly cold nights, greater numbers may roost in one box. There are several records of 16 and 17 birds roosting in one box and one record of 25 birds in one box.

Occasionally, people who monitor bluebird trails in winter find bluebirds that have died in the bottom of the boxes. In some cases this may be a result of too many birds roosting in one box, causing the bottom birds to suffocate, although there is no proof of this.

Bluebirds may use several roosting boxes in the course of a winter. Their location in early and midwinter may be nearer sources of berries and in late winter closer to nest boxes where the birds

have bred in the past, possibly as a preamble to claiming the box for the breeding season.

There are several ways to tell if bluebirds are roosting in your nest boxes. The first and most obvious is to see them enter or leave at night or in the morning. They tend to enter just before dusk and leave in the morning in the hour after sunrise. You may also look into your boxes during the day and find berry seeds in the base of the box, or droppings with seeds. This strongly suggests that bluebirds have roosted there.

And finally, of course, you can go out and monitor your boxes at night, taking care not to disturb the birds, since if disturbed they may not return to the box that night. The safest way to monitor at night is with a small dentist's mirror or similar tool and a penlight flashlight. The mirror is placed in through the hole and the flashlight shone into the box; you should be able to see the birds reflected in the mirror. Be sure to exercise the utmost care in doing this and stop if it seems to disturb the birds.

OTHER ASPECTS OF BLUEBIRD LIFE

Molts of Bluebirds

Young bluebirds are born with little bits of feathers called natal down. This is quickly replaced by the juvenal plumage, which starts to appear in the first few days of nestling life. This juvenal plumage is the typical plumage of fledgling birds that are just out of the nest and have not yet gone through a molt. It is best recognized by the spotting on the breast, similar to the spotted breast of young robins. In fact, this shows the close relationship between bluebirds and other members of the Turdidae (thrush) family.

As noted, once the young are on their own and no longer fed by the adults, they are just called juveniles. In mid- to late summer these juvenile birds will molt all of their body feathers, but keep

A male eastern bluebird entering a nest that has one albino nestling.

their wing and tail feathers. Birds born early in the season will start this molt as early as the beginning of July, while birds born in later broods may not start until mid-August. This molt is completed by fall. At that time, the birds will look almost identical to the adults and are now called adults.

For the rest of their lives they will have one molt per year, and this will occur in late summer and fall. It will involve the gradual replacement of *all* their feathers — their body feathers *and* wing and tail feathers.

Just after their molt in fall, adult bluebirds look slightly paler and not as brilliant a blue as in summer. This is because their body feathers are finely tipped with brownish edges. As the winter progresses, these edges wear off, making the birds look a brighter blue. This is especially noticeable in the males.

Albino Bluebirds

Rarely, bluebirds are seen with varying amounts of white on them. If they are totally white with pink eyes, then they are called abino. If they have just patches of white or lighter-colored feathers where they are normally dark, then the birds are called leucistic.

Both albino and leucistic individuals have been seen among eastern and western bluebirds. Leucistic birds have been seen among mountain bluebirds, but there have been very few albinos reported in this species.

Interestingly, among birds of the world, albinism is most commonly seen in the American robin which, again, is in the same family as the bluebirds — the thrush family.

Albinism is the result of a genetic defect that stops the process of pigment production. The eyes of an albino bird look pink because they lack pig-

A female eastern bluebird enjoying a bath.

ment, allowing the blood from the blood vessels in the eyes to show through.

Albino birds have trouble surviving because their feathers are weaker, and because they may be chased or harassed by members of their own species.

Bathing

Birds differ in the way that they bathe. Some birds, such as chickadees, just toss little droplets of water on their back with a flip of their bill. Other birds, like grackles, may get chest high in the water and flutter their wings. Then there are birds, such as bluebirds, that really get into bathing, settling down in the water, fluttering their wings and tail so that water sprays in all directions, and even sticking their head into the water.

Setting up a shallow birdbath near your bluebirds can be very attractive to them and fun for you to watch.

Pecking at Glass and Mirrors

People often discover bluebirds pecking at mirrors on cars or at windows of houses, and they wonder why the birds do it.

This behavior is not restricted to bluebirds but occurs in cardinals, titmice, and robins, among others. It is done by both male and female, generally during the breeding season.

To understand this behavior you have to take the bird's point of view. When the bluebird visits the mirror, it sees another bluebird of the same sex. Its first reaction is to chase it or peck at it. But every time it does this, the other bird seems to retaliate. If the bird goes to another mirror or window, then the intruder shows up there as well.

Birds do not understand that this is only a reflection but think it is another bird. Under natural conditions, pecking at another bird makes it go away. But in this case it does not have that effect.

Thus, from the bird's point of view, this whole situation is unusual and continues to stimulate

A male eastern bluebird that may be "closer than it appears."

its aggressive behavior. The only way to stop it is to cover up the mirror or glass wherever the bluebird is pecking. Once the bird has stopped visiting the spot, you can remove the cover.

The Life Span of Bluebirds

The first few months of a bluebird's life are the hardest because the bird must survive in a dangerous world with very little experience of gathering food and avoiding danger. Because of this, it is estimated that about 50 percent of fledglings do not make it through this stage of life.

If a bluebird lives through the fledgling stage, then it has a good chance of living to be about 2–3 years old. This is probably the average life span of a bluebird. There are very few records to help us determine bluebird longevity, but those that exist suggest that bluebirds, with luck, can live up to 10 years in the wild.

RESOURCES

Books, Journals, and Newsletters About Bluebirds

Bluebird News (newsletter). Box 1624, Mount Pleasant, TX 75455.

Braun, Katharine. 1982. *Saga of the Bluebird*. Pompano Beach, FL: Exposition Press.

Brunell, Dr. Shirl. 1988. *I Hear Bluebirds*. New York: Vantage Press.

Dew, Tina and Curtis, and R. B. Leighton. 1986. *Bluebirds: Their Daily Lives and How to Attract and Raise Bluebirds*. Jackson, MS: Nature Book Publishers.

Dion, Andre P. 1984. *The Return of the Bluebird*. St-Placide, Quebec: Editions Auto-Correct-Art Inc.

Gutzke, Theodore W. 1985. *A Bibliography on the Technical Literature of the Bluebird Genus Sialia*. Silver Spring, MD: North American Bluebird Society.

Scriven, Dorene. 1989. *Bluebirds in the Upper Midwest: A Guide to Successful Trail Management*. Minneapolis, MN: Bluebird Recovery Committee, Audubon Chapter of Minneapolis.

Shantz, B. 1986. *Mountain Bluebird Management*. Lacombe, Alberta: Deer Ridge Consulting Ltd.

Shantz, B., and M. Pearman. 1984. *Nest Boxes for Alberta Birds*. Red Deer, Alberta: Ellis Bird Farm.

Sialia, The Quarterly Journal of the North American Bluebird Society (all issues). Published by the North American Bluebird Society, Silver Spring, MD 20906.

Stokes, Donald W., and Lillian Q. Stokes. 1989. *A Guide to Bird Behavior*. Vol. 3. Boston: Little, Brown.

———. 1990. *The Complete Birdhouse Book*. Boston: Little, Brown.

Zeleny, Lawrence. 1978. *The Bluebird: How You Can Help Its Fight for Survival*. Bloomington: Indiana University Press.

Videos

Backyard Blues by Boz Metzdorf, Birds Eye View Productions.

Bluebird Trails by Boz Metzdorf, Birds Eye View Productions.

Bluebirds Up Close by Michael Godfrey, Nature Science Network.

Jewels of Blue by Boz Metzdorf, Birds Eye View Productions.

Manufacturers of Birdhouses

Ahlgren Construction Company, 14017 White Rock Rd., Burnsville, MN 55337.

Aspects, Inc., 245 Child St., P.O. Box 408, Warren, RI 02885.

Audubon Workshop, Inc., 1501 Paddock Dr., Northbrook, IL 60062.

The Bird House, P.O. Box 722, Estacada, OR 97023.

Briggs Associates, Inc., 851–A4 Highway 224, Denver, CO 80229.

C&S Products, Inc., Box 848, Fort Dodge, IA 50501.

Chesapeake Creative Arts, P.O. Box 444, Riderwood, MD 21139.

Country Ecology, P.O. Box 59, Center Sandwich, NH 03227.

Dan Ogle's Mountain Crafts, Rt. 2, Box 194A, Huskey's Grove Rd., Sevierville, TN 37862.

Dennis Thaden Company, 455 Harrison St. N.E., Minneapolis, MN 55413.

Duncraft, 33 Fisherville Rd., Penacook, NH 03303-9020.

Heath Manufacturing Co., 140 Mill St., Coopersville, MI 49404.

Holland's Woodworks, P.O. Box 69, Powers, OR 97466.

Hyde Bird Feeder Company, P.O. Box 168, Waltham, MA 02254.

Kellogg Inc., 322 East Florida St., Milwaukee, WI 53201.

Kinsman Co., River Road, Point Pleasant, PA 18950.

Marsh Creek, P.O. Box 928, Geneva, NY 14456.

May Engineering, P.O. Box 351, Troy, MO 63379.

North American Bluebird Society, Box 6295, Silver Spring, MD 20906.

North States Industries, Inc., 1200 Mendelssohn Ave., Suite 210, Minneapolis, MN 55427.

Northwest Birdhouse Company, 4155 North Chase Rd., Rathdrum, ID 83858.

Opus, P.O. Box 525, Bellingham, MA 02019.

Pennington Enterprises, Inc., P.O. Box 290, Madison, GA 30650.

Rubbermaid, Inc., 1147 Akron Rd., Wooster, OH 44691.

Salt Creek Birdhouses, 452 North Walnut, Wood Dale, IL 60191.

Towanda Bird House, 6405 E. Kellogg, Wichita, KS 67207.

White's Birdhouse Company, 5153 Neff Lake Rd., Brooksville, FL 34601.

Retail Mail-Order Catalogs Specializing in Bird Products

Audubon Park Company, Drawer W, Akron, CO 80720.

Audubon Workshop, Inc., 1501 Paddock Dr., Northbrook, IL 60062.

Barn Owl Gift Shop, 2509 Lakeshore Dr., Fennville, MI 49408.

The Brown Company, P.O. Box 277, Yagoo Pond Rd., West Kingston, RI 02892.

Canadian Nature Federation, 453 Sussex Dr., Ottawa, Ontario K1N 6Z4.

The Crow's Nest Bookshop, Laboratory of Ornithology at Cornell University, 159 Sapsucker Woods Rd., Ithaca, NY 14850.

Duncraft, 33 Fisherville Rd., Penacook, NH 03303.

Hyde Bird Feeder Company, P.O. Box 168, Waltham, MA 02254.

North American Bluebird Society, Box 6295, Silver Spring, MD 20906.

Ol' Sam Peabody Company, P.O. Box 316, Berrien Springs, MI 49103.

Wild Bird Supplies, 4815 Oak St., Crystal Lake, IL 60012.

The Wood Thrush Shop, 992 Davidson Dr., Nashville, TN 37205.

Predator Controls

Ahlgren Construction Company, 14017 White Rock Rd., Burnsville, MN 55337.

Audubon Workshop, Inc., 1501 Paddock Dr., Northbrook, IL 60062. Raccoon and snake guards, sparrow traps.

Bluebird Recovery Project, Audubon Chapter of Minneapolis, P.O. Box 566, Minneapolis, MN 55458. Information on sparrow traps.

Ellis Bird Farm, Box 2980, Lacombe, Alberta, T0C 1S0. Information on sparrow and starling traps and all types of nest boxes.

Harry Krueger, Rt. 2, Box OR28, Ore City, TX 75683. Will send you plans for snake guard if you send self-addressed, legal-size envelope with $.45 worth of stamps, and $1.00 to cover cost of diagrams.

Joseph Huber, 1720 Evergreen Ct., Heath, OH 43056. Information on sparrow traps.

North American Bluebird Society, Box 6295, Silver Spring, MD 20906. Sells sparrow traps.

Bluebird Societies

There is only one continent-wide bluebird organization and that is the North American Bluebird Society. In addition, there are many marvelous regional bluebird societies and organized bluebird trails all across North America. For a complete listing of all bluebird societies and organized bluebird trails, write to the North American Bluebird Society (Box 6295, Silver Spring, MD 20906) and ask for their North American Bluebird Trail Directory.